EMMANUEL GUIBERT

HOW THE WORLD WAS

A CALIFORNIA CHILDHOOD

First Second
New York

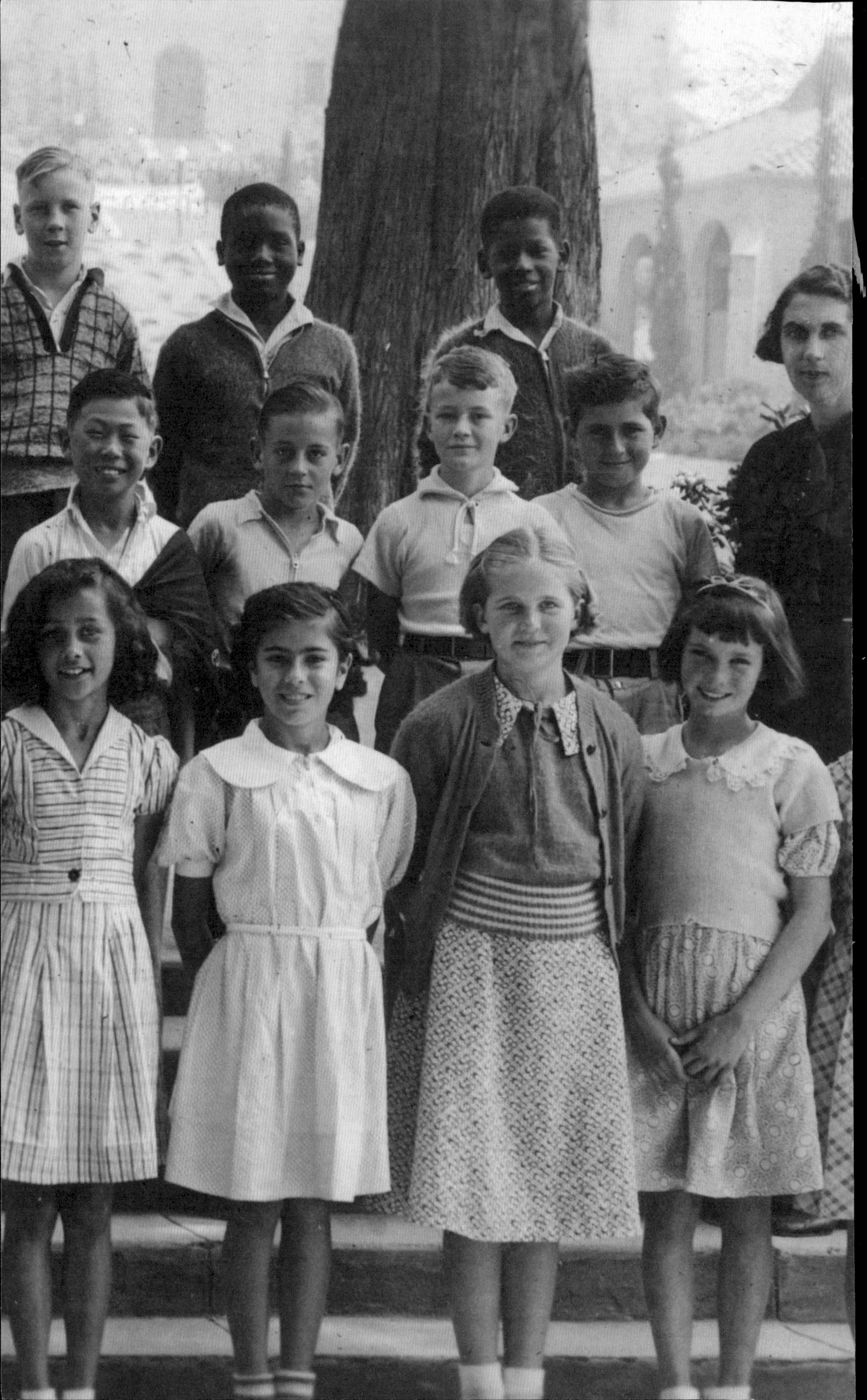

For Cecilia

So you want me to tell you a little bit about
my childhood in Southern California?

I have wondrous memories of my country before the war.

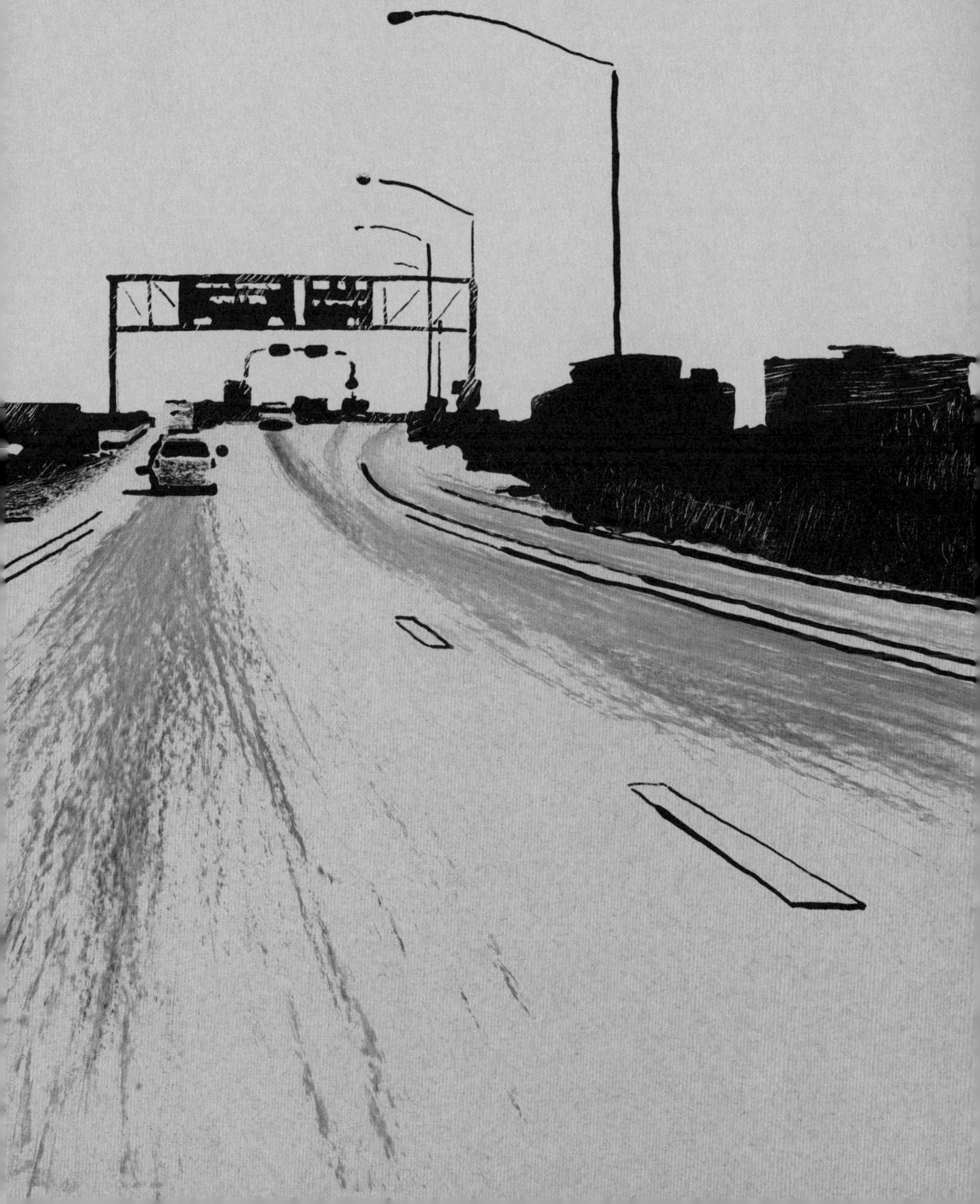

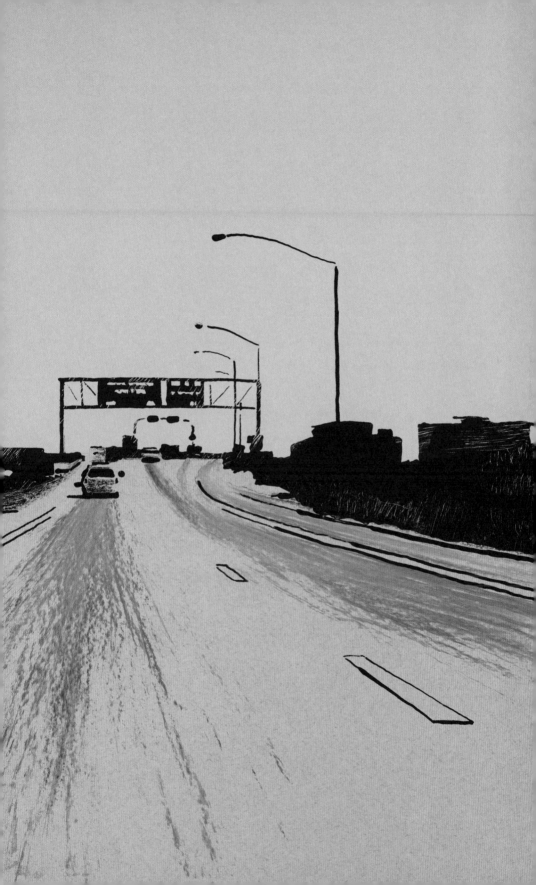

It was during the war that everything changed.

A tremendous number of people, soldiers, factory and
shipyard workers, spent time on the Pacific Coast.
A whole lot of people who knew nothing about California
passed through it.

After the war, which for us lasted four years, the
population had doubled.

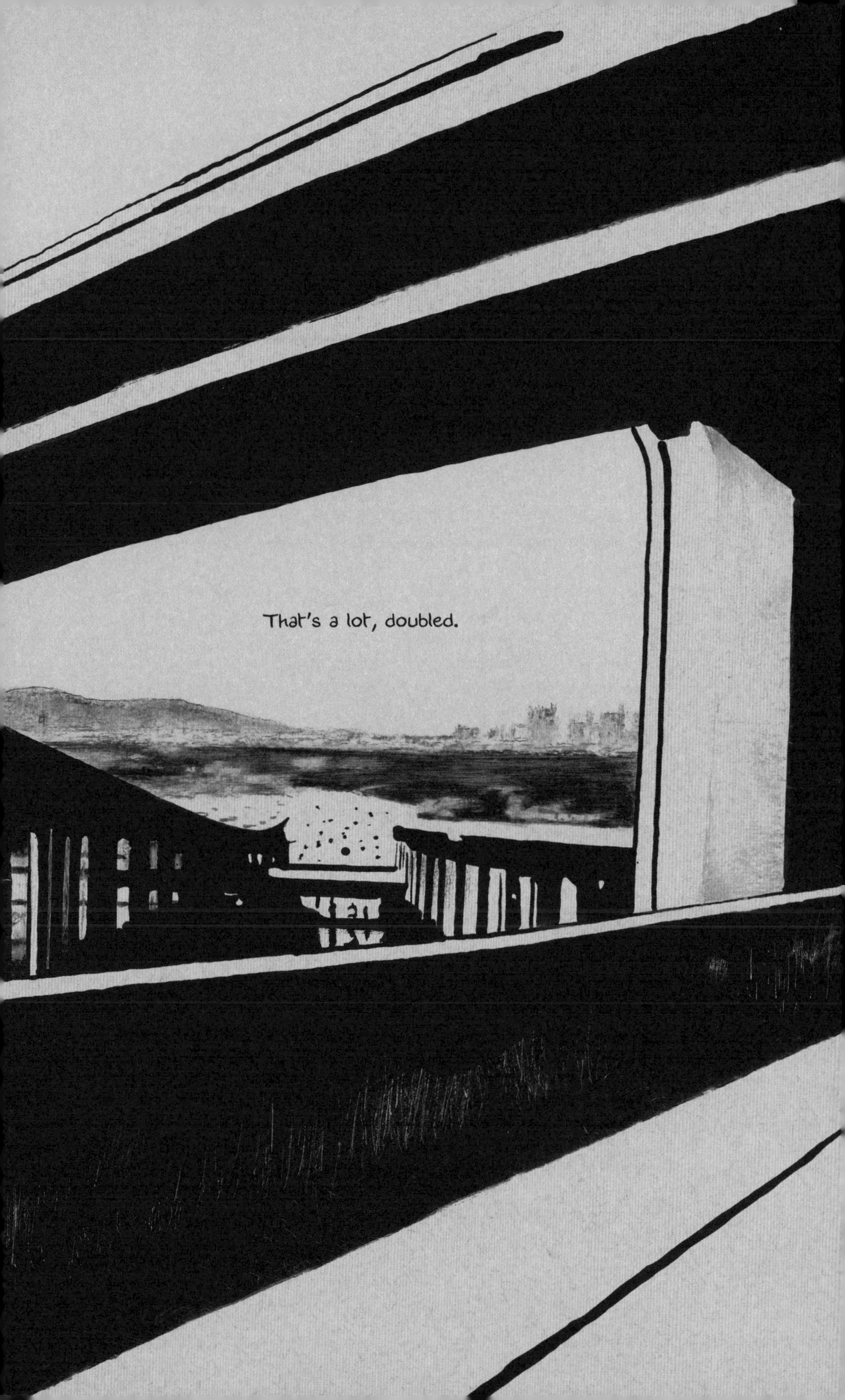
That's a lot, doubled.

Then came the smog.
Air pollution.
We'd never heard of the word "smog" before the war.
I had no idea such a thing could happen.

The air was clear and wonderful.
Nature, absolutely magnificent.

One city I really liked was Santa Barbara.
It's built up against the hills; behind them
were lemon groves.

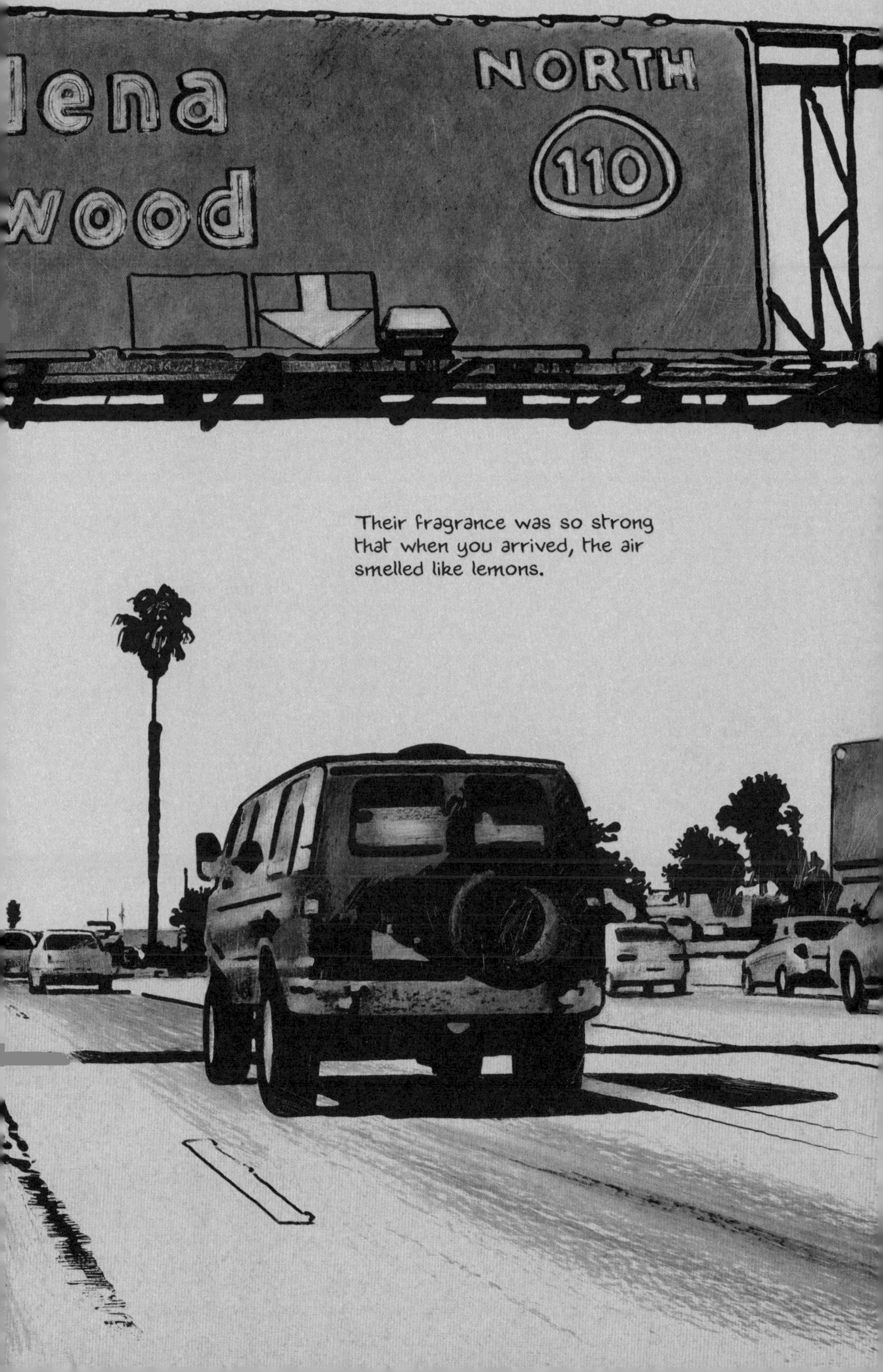
lena
wood
NORTH
110
Their fragrance was so strong that when you arrived, the air smelled like lemons.

From Los Angeles, you'd take the Camino Real to get to Santa Barbara.
The "royal road"—an ancient route that stretches from
San Diego all the way up to San Francisco.
Father Junipero Serra, a Spanish Franciscan monk, came up from Mexico
and founded twenty-one missions along the length of that road.
I don't remember when, exactly.
Those little missions are made of adobe bricks—dirt mixed with straw
that's pressed into a mold and left to bake in the sun.
They're very pretty.

There's San Juan Capistrano, made famous by the song:
"When the swallows come back to Capistrano,
I'll be waiting there for you."

The nicest one is in Santa Barbara.

After the padre's time, when they started to build a
road that could be used by horse-drawn vehicles,
the Camino Real's route stayed the same.

When cars came along, it didn't change.

Even today, in many places, it remains the same.

The Camino Real that I knew was a narrow road.
Many sections had only one lane.
The surface was in bad shape, and cars often broke down.

You passed through forests of those wonderful California oaks.
Very rich agricultural areas.
At night and early in the morning, you could hear the coyotes howling.
There were pumas, too.

Anyway, life was completely different then.

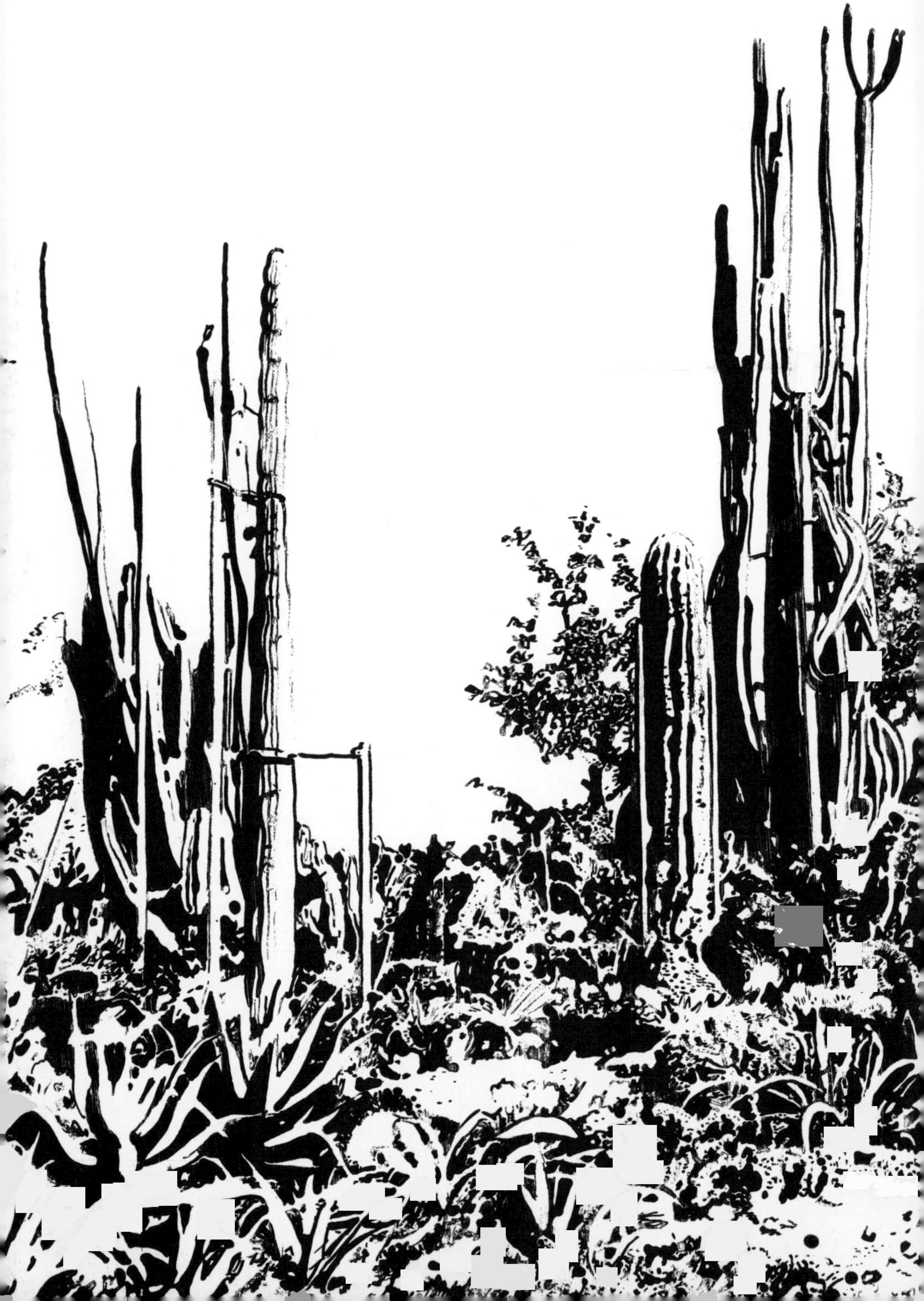

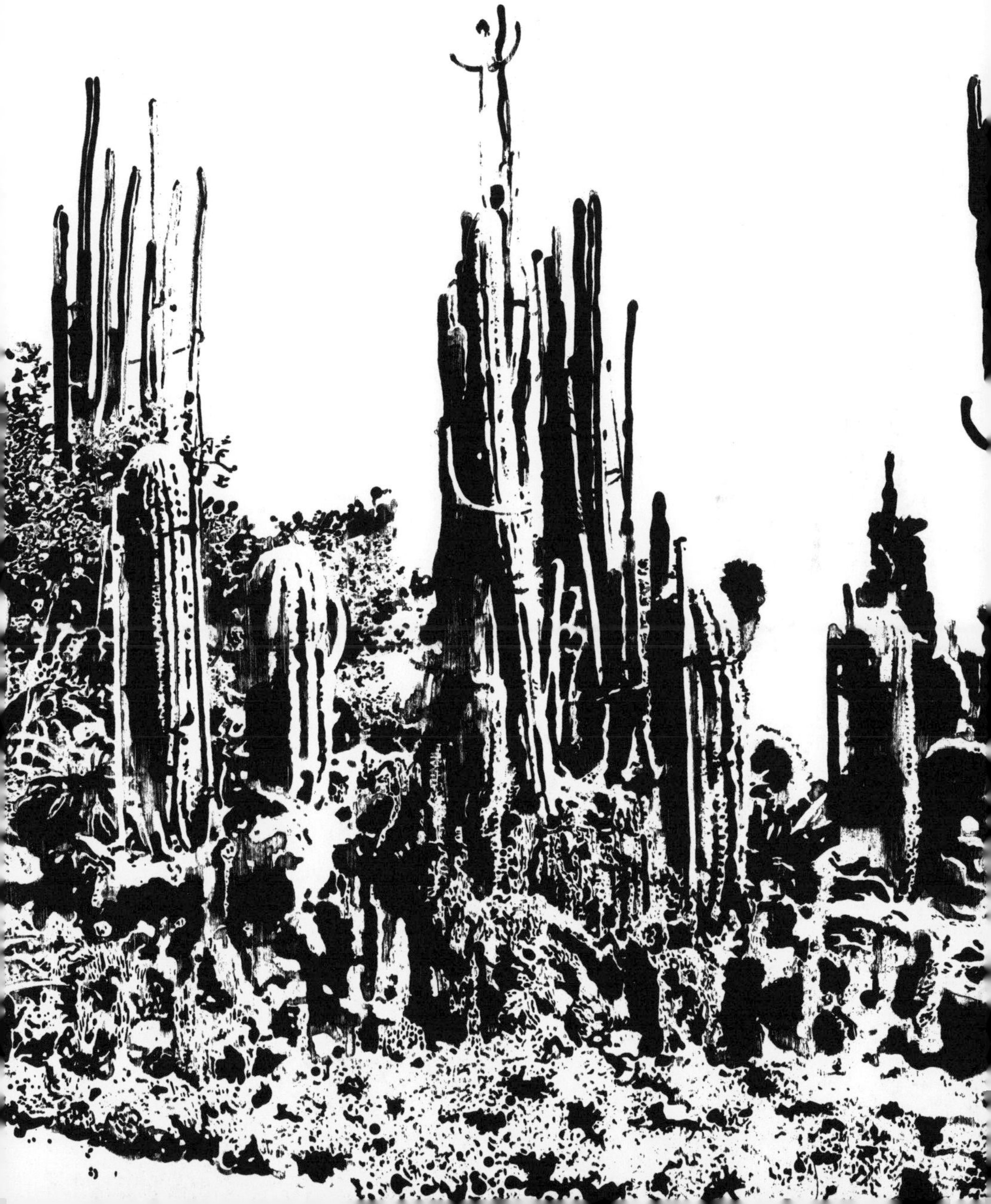

1

When I was a child, we lived in a series of different houses.
I counted them the other day; there were fourteen.

First I lived in Alhambra, where I was born in 1925 and which
became a sort of Los Angeles suburb.
I was very young then and don't remember much about it.

I remember dropping a scoop of ice cream onto the
ground because I wouldn't hold the cone straight.
My father had bought it for me; it fell on the sidewalk,
into some fresh cement.
Workmen were busy nearby.

I have some vague memories of my father from early childhood.
He was always very busy.
I never really found out what his own childhood was like.
Of him as a child, adolescent, and young adult,
I know almost nothing.

I think he was about four when he and his family moved from the East Coast to the West Coast. He grew up in San Jose, just south of San Francisco.

In fact, that's where he met the girl who'd become his wife. Esther Elizabeth Hanson; her nickname was Bunny.

One day, in front of my maternal grandparents' house, my father was wrestling on the lawn with one of my mother's brothers. The brother was a year or two older than Bunny, but people thought he was younger, because he was small and skinny.

Bunny came running. She thought my father was fighting with her brother for real and jumped him.

They fought hard, physically.
She won. Or maybe he let her win,
that's a lot more likely; he was
pretty tough.
That's how they met.

I don't know how long it was from
the time they met until they got
married. I don't know any details
about the marriage.

My father began a course of studies in applied arts and crafts, which
was interrupted by his service in the navy during the First World War.
The war ended before he was sent into combat.
He had two years to go to complete his bachelor of arts degree,
but he had to wait until he could borrow some money.
In the meantime, I was born.

When I was three or so, we moved to Santa Barbara,
where my father finished up his studies at California State University.
That's what it was called at the time.

There, we lived in two different houses.
The first was very small, in back of a bigger one.

One day, a little girl I used to play with gave me some seeds to eat
that turned out to be poisonous.

I started throwing up.
They called the doctor; after questioning me
he figured out what it was that I had eaten.
I can still see myself lying there sick, in a little bed
with sides that went up and down.
It didn't kill me, but I did have a delicate stomach
for a few years.

At the age of seventeen, it was my turn to come back to Santa Barbara to study at the university.

I was able, without the slightest hesitation, to head straight to the street where that house was and find it right away.

Later, when I was four, we moved to another house, higher up. It was built on a very steep slope; the entrance was on the second floor.

The back yards were adjoining, with no separation between them.
Our neighbors had irises, lots of irises.
Snails love irises.

One day, I decided to get a bucket and go snail-hunting.
Definitely not to eat them.
At the time, we Americans didn't eat them.
I just liked them, that's all.

I filled the bucket with snails.
There were tons of them, and I left the bucket in the middle of the kitchen.
It was fairly early in the morning.
After that, I went off to do something or other.

At around noon, my mother went into the kitchen to fix lunch;
suddenly I heard her shriek in horror.
The snails, of course, hadn't stayed in the bucket.

She scolded me, but not too hard.
The snails were climbing everywhere; I helped her pry them off
the furniture and the walls.
I remember it all clearly; I never did it again.

It's not easy for me to describe my mother physically.

I don't think you could have called her beautiful. She had a pleasant appearance.
Her face was always a little tired-looking, even when she was young.

She wore little or no makeup.
It's not that she was against it, but we didn't have any money, and I think she just didn't see the need to buy such things.
Anyway, at the time, a lot of women didn't wear makeup.
It was just starting then.

Her breasts sagged a bit.

She'd talk about the times she had to run races in high school P.E., and how her friends who also had heavy breasts would tape them down so that they wouldn't go SLAP SLAP.

She thought: "I'm not going to tape them down; it'll just pull on the skin and be painful. I'll be able to run faster if I just let them go SLAP SLAP."
And she'd win those races.

She wasn't a very good cook, because neither family was of an epicurean bent, and during the Great Depression, in 1929, we never ate anything expensive.

She liked to dress well.
She was very sweet; everybody loved her.

She wore her hair in the latest style, which at the time wasn't too difficult.
She had a curling iron that she'd heat up on the gas stove.
She'd slip a piece of toilet paper in between the two pieces of metal and if it didn't scorch, it meant that the iron wouldn't burn her hair.

She often made her own clothes. The fashions of the time weren't particularly attractive. A lot of the clothes were very—how should I put it—very loose. Blouses that weren't tight.

She was fairly short.

She had allergies.
The doctors did test after test,
but they couldn't figure out
what it was she was allergic to.
Finally, they decided it was
horsehair.

But horses? There were no
horses nearby. Someone thought
to cut open our mattresses.
Inside was a mix of wool and
horsehair.

She loved music, though she wasn't
a singer. I don't remember her
singing much. She liked the songs
of Stephen Foster. Stephen Foster
was a white man interested in black
music who wrote a whole lot of
popular songs.

She had two favorite songs: "Flow
Gently, Sweet Afton" and "Jeanie
with the Light Brown Hair."

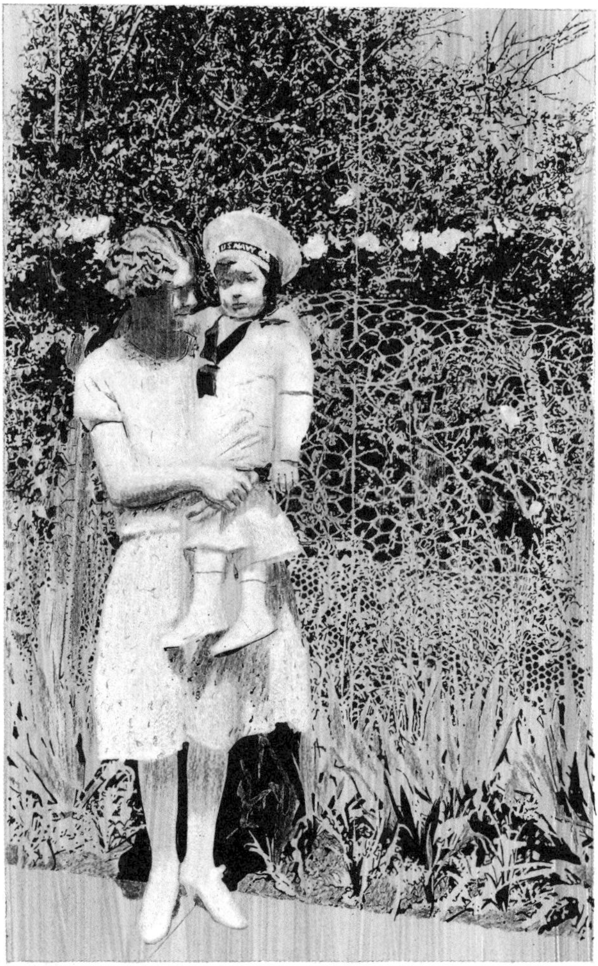
U.S. NAVY

2

Once my father had finished his studies, we moved back to Alhambra, where my Cope grandparents lived. It was the middle of the Depression. The only work my father could find was as a stockboy in a grocery store.

My grandfather Cope was always cold. He suffered from a duodenal ulcer.
He had to work for a living, like so many other poor people in the 1930s who had no pension or Social Security, just their small salary. He'd come home in the evenings, settle down in his armchair, turn up the space heater, and stay there, trying to warm up. No one thought to ration his use of the space heater; that's just what he did.

In those days, if you had money, you went to the doctor. If you didn't, you didn't. You just stayed sick and waited to die.

The only luxury my father allowed himself was to treat us, on rare occasions, to a malted milk at a small soda fountain on Alhambra's Main Street.

Watching him sit there drinking the shake through a big straw, you could see that he was thoroughly enjoying it. It was a bit too much for me, but he was always able to finish mine, too.

By some miracle, he found work at a school, John Marshall Junior High, on Allen Avenue in Pasadena. It was a substitute teacher job that later became a permanent one. He stayed there his whole life.

A lathe operator, he taught metal shop, electric shop, machine tool shop, foundry, auto shop, all those sorts of things.

He rented an almost-new house on a quiet street in Alhambra, a municipality north of Pasadena. It was probably a bit too expensive for us, which is why we didn't stay there long.

We had an extra room we didn't need. My mother rented it out to a man with very dark hair, a bachelor we hardly ever saw. He had a machine that sharpened safety-razor blades. Those razors, which were fitted with small rectangular blades, were still a novelty and the blades were fairly expensive, so our renter sharpened them. Sometimes he'd let me turn the handle of the machine.

Next door there were children I used to play with. We'd head for a nearby vacant lot. California cities were full of vacant lots in those days.

California pepper trees grew there. We called them pepper trees, but they weren't really. After they bloom, they produce seeds that have a very peppery taste, but it's not a good idea to eat them.
Long stalks covered with tiny leaves hang down from the ends of their branches, all the way to the ground. They look a bit like weeping willows.

The other kids and I would grab a bunch of stalks in each hand, tie a big double knot and make a swing out of them.

The only thing is, those trees ooze a gluey kind of sap that sticks to your hands and clothes and quickly turns black.

I can't count the times I got into trouble because of those pepper tree swings!
My mother had trouble washing both the clothes and the boy, but I loved that game.

Plus, the sap smelled really good.

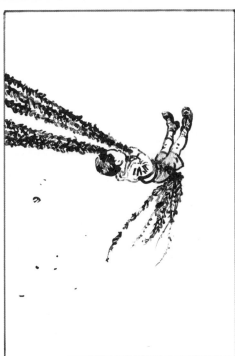

At that time, we were just starting to see a lot more planes in the sky—monoplanes, biplanes, and even triplanes.
There was an airfield nearby. Some of the planes did acrobatics, loop de loops or dives, or flew upside down.

If you were home and heard the sound of a small plane, you'd run outside to see it.

That shows it was still something very special, I think.

I started kindergarten there. I went to the primary school at the end of the street.

One day in school they asked us to recite and act out a fairy tale or a nursery rhyme. I chose:

Humpty Dumpty.

Humpty Dumpty sat on a wall.
Humpty Dumpty had a great fall.
All the king's horses and all the king's men
Couldn't put Humpty together again.

I thought: "To be just like Humpty, I have to have a great fall."

I knocked myself right out. They carried me home and explained to my mother that I had thrown myself to the ground headfirst.

3

I first encountered the idea of God at the age of five, because of a
laundry room, my penis, a sewing needle, my mother, and a hornet. This is a true
and serious story that has a lesson for whoever will listen.
Not that the same thing could happen to somebody else, but similar things
can happen.

Under the back half of our house was a basement area that consisted
of a hallway, a good-sized room where you could hang laundry to dry,
and another room with two utility sinks, with running water.
In the larger of the two rooms was a central-heating gas boiler.
It was the only house we ever lived in that had central heating.

The hot air circulated through all the rooms in the house
through vents you could open or close. The vent openings
were covered by grates.
I was fascinated by those grates.
Actually, the whole idea of heating systems fascinated me.

One day, I was in the laundry room with my mother, who had just given me a bath in one of the big sinks where she did the laundry.

She dried me off, sat me down on her lap and started to clean my penis in a strange kind of way, using the blunt end of a sewing needle. At that stage I was already circumcised. She ran the needle back and forth through the tiny folds in the skin.

She tried to explain the concept of circumcision to me as best she could, but I didn't understand much of what she said.

The doctor who delivered you didn't circumcise you properly. It got slightly infected where the skin was sewn up after it was cut.

The procedure had left little openings about a millimeter long just under the epidermis. She'd run the blunt end of the needle through them to remove the stuff that had accumulated there from baths, sweat, and flaking skin.

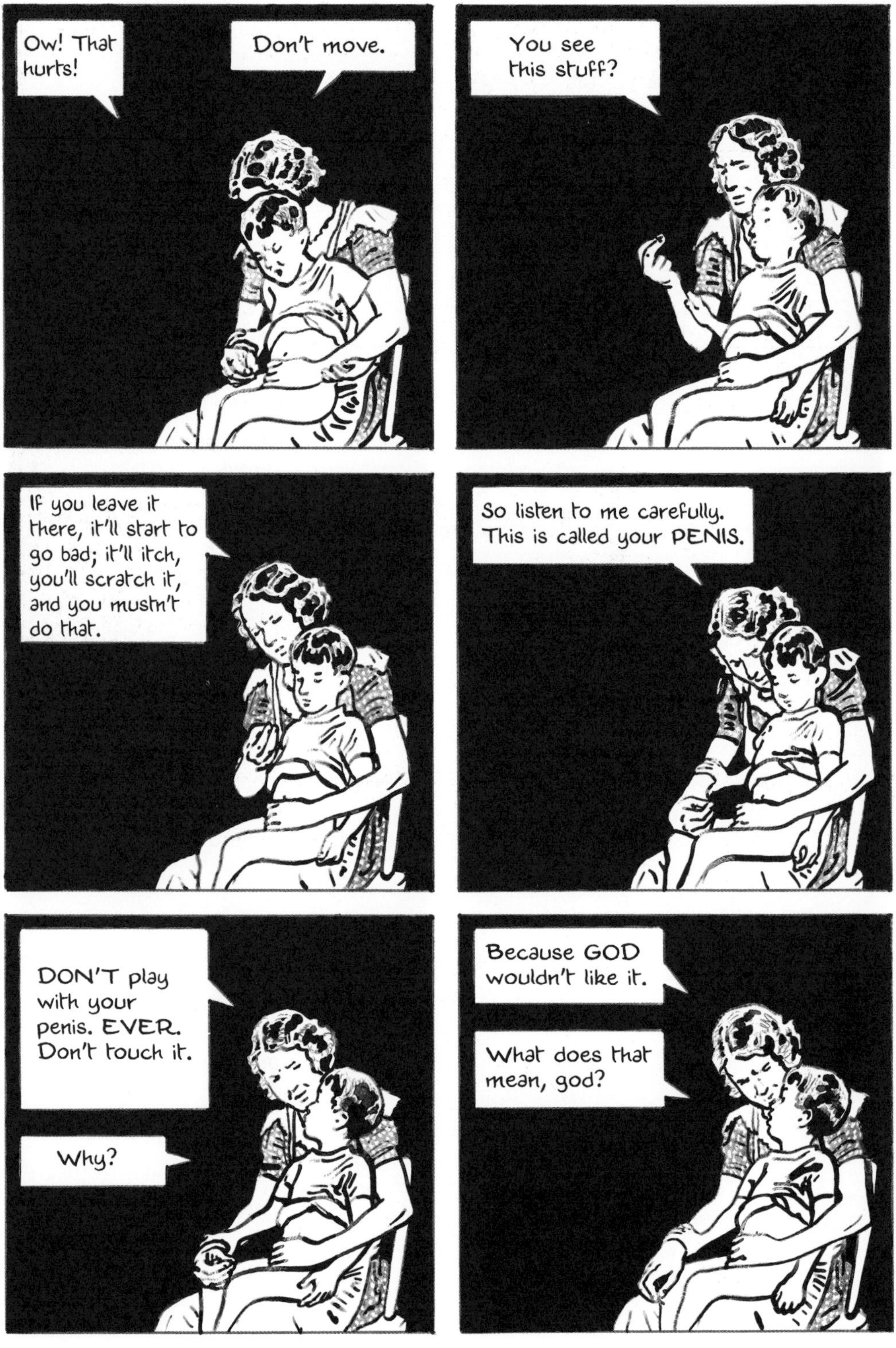
Ow! That hurts!
Don't move.
You see this stuff?
If you leave it there, it'll start to go bad; it'll itch, you'll scratch it, and you mustn't do that.
So listen to me carefully. This is called your PENIS.
DON'T play with your penis. EVER. Don't touch it.
Why?
Because GOD wouldn't like it.
What does that mean, god?

I remember it as if it were yesterday.

We didn't really speak about it again. Actually, I'm pretty sure we NEVER spoke of it again.

I decided on the spot to do what she had said.

As for God,
the subject did resurface in the conversation; I'll explain later.

Some time after that, in the middle of the night, when I was asleep in my little room, I was awakened by an awful sound.

I had no idea what it was. It came and went.

ZOOM ZOOM

As if an invisible plane had entered the room and was flying right next to my bed.

I was absolutely terrified. I screamed.

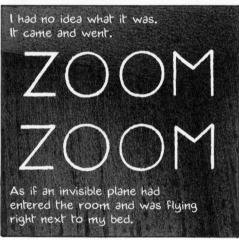

My parents came running. Even they were a bit confused by the sound. Then my father said:

It's a hornet.

He's trapped behind the heating grate. I don't know how he got in there. The sound is echoing through the duct, that's what's making that noise.

I'll get rid of him. Calm down and go to sleep. It's not dangerous.

I screamed and screamed and screamed. I was beside myself.

I didn't know what a hornet was.
I thought it was the voice of the heating vent whose depths I could never see into—that big, mysterious hole that scared me.

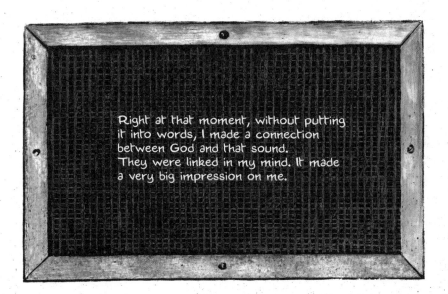

Right at that moment, without putting it into words, I made a connection between God and that sound.
They were linked in my mind. It made a very big impression on me.

My father went down to the basement.
He did something or other and got rid of the hornet.

I can still see the whole scene clearly. Even at my age, I can still hear all the words, and I can still hear that sound.

After we left that house and moved into the next one, my parents sent me to Sunday school at the Altadena Protestant Presbyterian Church.

Every Sunday morning at 11 o'clock, while the grownups attended church services, the children went to Sunday school. It lasted for an hour.
We little kids made paper cutouts and collages, played games, and drew pictures; someone would tell us Bible stories, very simple ones.
It was a kind of initiation.
We learned about Jesus and God, Jesus's father, the creator of all things and all people. The protestant church avoids displaying images in God's likeness.

I hadn't forgotten about God, and I thought: "Good thing I don't touch my penis, because here's this gentleman again. I have to stay careful so that he doesn't get upset."

The idea that my mother had put into my head stayed with me. I think its impact wouldn't have been as great if it hadn't been for the hornet and the fear it triggered. Even though they kept explaining to me that a hornet was only a big bee, I just couldn't make the connection between bees, which I was very familiar with, and that horrible sound. The hornet sealed the pact between God and me right then and there.

So for the rest of my childhood and during my adolescence and young adulthood, I kept the habit of never touching my penis, except to wash and to pee, and even then I did so as little as possible. It became automatic. It was part of my way of being.

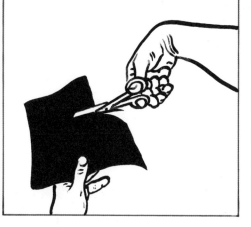

When I saw other boys shaking their penises in every direction to get rid of the last drop, I'd think: "Hmm, they sure touch theirs a lot."

I got to an age where I wanted to masturbate.
I found all sorts of ways to do it. I masturbated quite effectively and even, I'd say, frequently, but never with my hands. That became second nature for me.

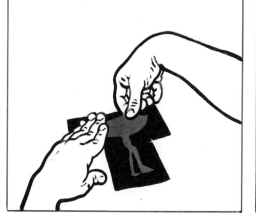

After I got married, when making love I touched my penis as little as possible. Sometimes it's necessary, but generally speaking I managed in other ways. I didn't even think about it. That strange discipline had become a habit.

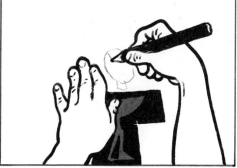

One day, I don't know why, when I was well into adulthood, I became aware of my discomfort at the idea of touching my genitals. I didn't mind touching women's genitals; I touched them the way any man would. It didn't bother me at all. The notion was limited to my own genitals, always with the idea of not displeasing God, even though I no longer belonged to a church and in fact had become more of a pagan, with other ideas about religion.

That day, in midlife, I thought:
"Well, it's pretty silly, the way I've been living up to now."
So I started to use my hands.

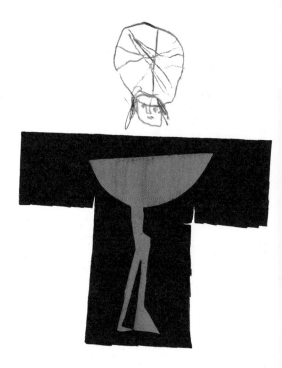

This story's a bit embarrassing to tell, but I think it's an excellent example of what can happen when you put patently absurd ideas into a small child's head. They can remain anchored in the personality permanently and, most importantly, at the unconscious level.

You can apply this to situations that have nothing to do with sex, although sex is a very important part of people's lives, even for people who don't consciously realize it.

4

There's a street in Altadena, Santa Rosa Avenue, that everyone called "Christmas Tree Lane." In earlier days it had been the entrance road to a huge ranch. It was a mile long.

It was very steep.
On either side was a deep, wide ditch to catch the runoff from the mountain when it rained; the houses were accessible by little bridges.

Both sides of the road were lined with deodar cedars, a very beautiful type of conifer. The bottom branches curved up like pagoda roofs, or the brim of a hat.
A deodar's needles are long, fat, and gray-green.
The color an elephant would be if it were green.

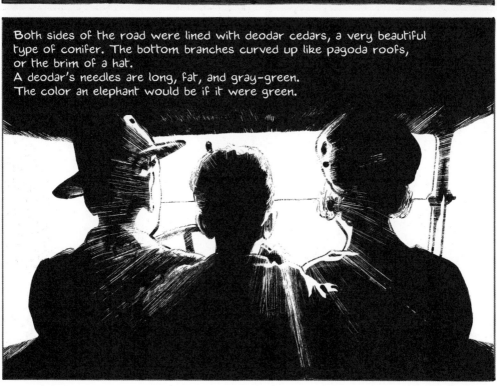

Before Christmas, the electric company and firemen from all over the area would string those enormous trees with garlands of Christmas lights.
People came from hundreds of miles away to see them.
We'd proceed slowly up the avenue, by car or on foot.
It was amazing to be strolling along under gigantic Christmas trees.

And when you got to the end, you could see the moon shining on the mountain.

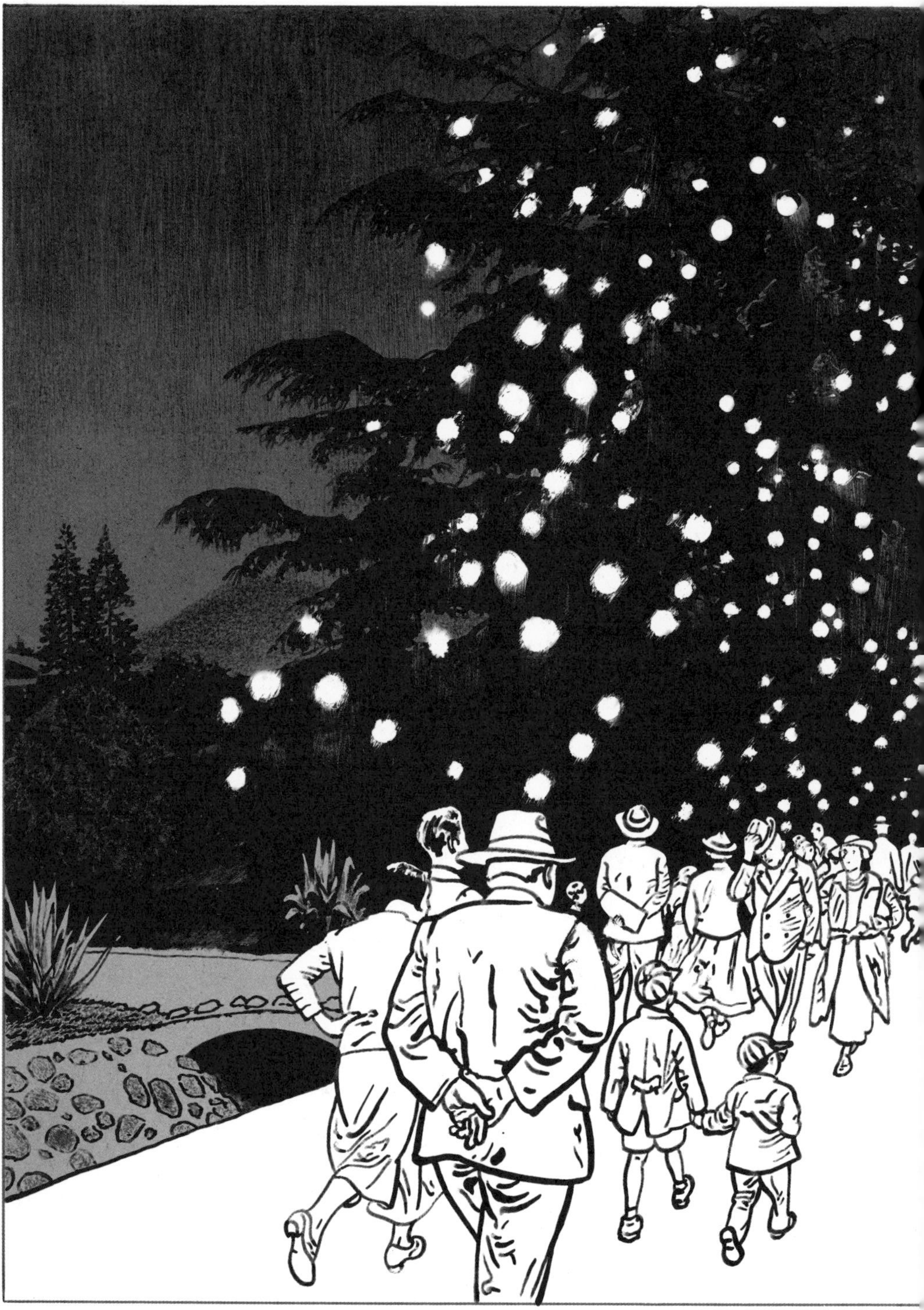

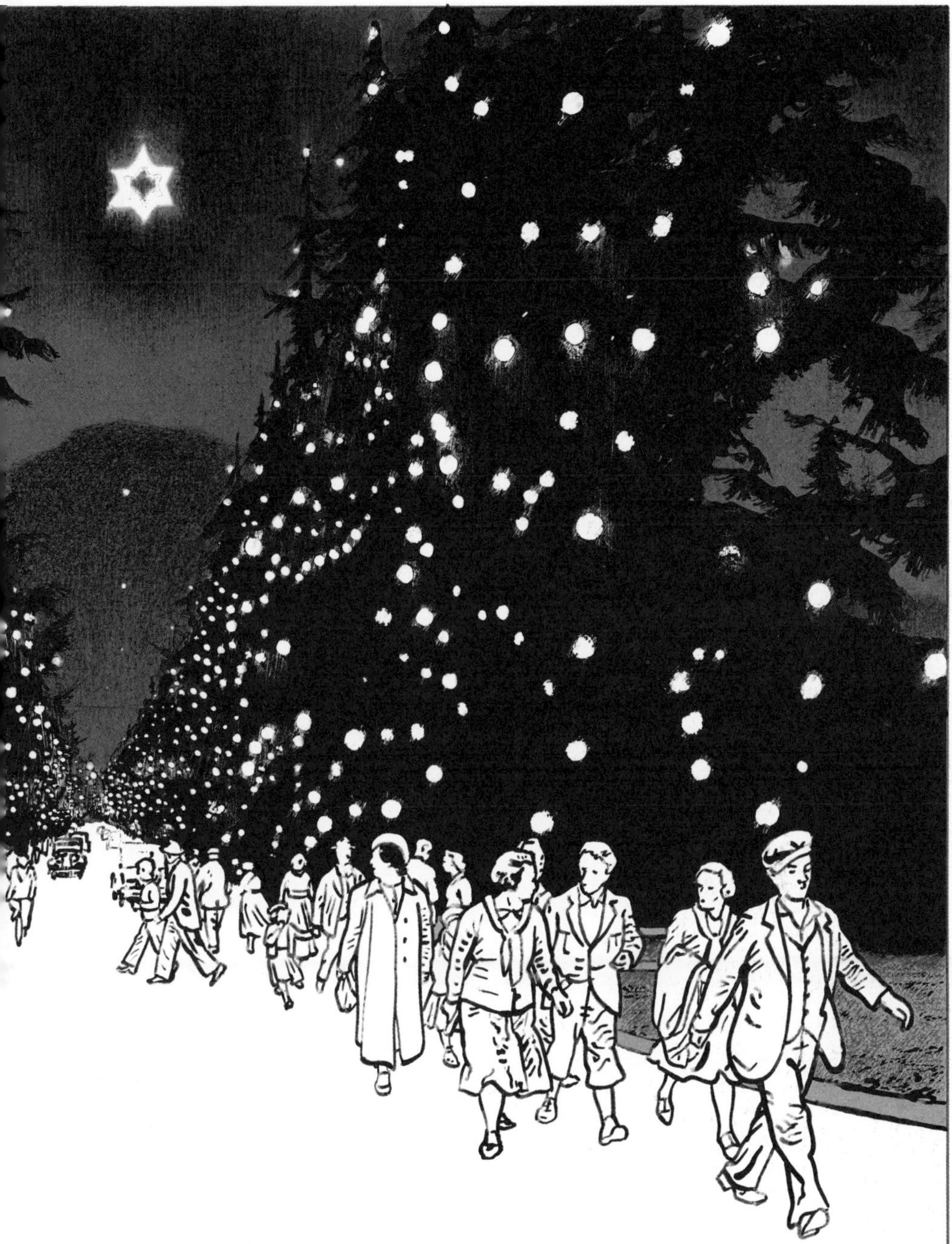

Every four years or so, powerful winds swept through the area. Not just wind gusts, but winds that regularly reached 160 miles an hour, without interruption. It was terrifying. People protected themselves as best they could.

During one of those windstorms, the worst that I ever experienced, a nearby house lost its roof. It was a beautiful wood house, recently built. The roof flew off all in one piece and landed gently in a nearby vacant lot. Later on, they were able to put it right back on.

That storm uprooted a lot of trees, especially black acacias around a certain age, about fifty years old. They weren't able to withstand the wind, and hundreds of them toppled over, all across the city. The acacias had provided a lot of shade.

At the time, we lived in a shabby little house tucked behind an expensive house, on Mariposa Avenue in Altadena. People would often put up a shack in the back of their property to rent out, because the lots were so big.
We did have a small garden, though. My mother set out a table and two wicker chairs.

During the big windstorm, they blew away.

A few months later, my mother recognized her furniture on a porch a few blocks away. She knocked on the door.

Ma'am, I think this furniture is mine. The wind blew it away during the storm.

Oh! That's very possible. We found it in the street.

My mother and that woman became friends.

My father, who was an excellent auto mechanic, always managed
to find old cars to fix up.
Sometimes we'd go to the beach on Saturday or Sunday or during
school vacations.
Pasadena and Altadena are about thirty miles from the coast. We'd drive
to Long Beach, which is the name of both a beach and a city.

We'd drive through oil fields.
An oil well might belong to an individual or to a company.
The wells pumped oil twenty-four hours a day, pump pump pump, up,
down, up, down; there was a strong smell of sulfur. It was an interesting
scene, very dirty.

Sometimes we'd take the highway to Santa Monica.
My parents preferred Long Beach, which was a wilder area.
But the hilly road from Los Angeles to Santa Monica had its own charm.

The smell of the Pacific Ocean permeated the air. Ten miles before we got to the coast, all of a sudden we could smell the ocean.

The car windows would be open, because it was nice out, and we'd always say:

There! You can smell the ocean!

We'd finally arrive at those long beaches of fine white sand.
They were fairly wide; it was a long walk to the water.
That part of the coast had quite a small tidal range.

We'd always pick a spot a good distance from the shore. My father
preferred it that way.

He hardly ever went into the water. He didn't like it.
It's true that the Pacific Ocean is much colder than the Atlantic. Even in
summer when the weather's boiling hot, the water never gets even lukewarm.

In my earliest memories, I was too young to know how to swim.
I had to be watched, but I was obedient.
If I was told not to go in past my knees, I'd stop when the water
got to mid-thigh.

In those days, swimsuits were made of wool jersey; they were itchy and scratchy.
When sand got inside them, it was very uncomfortable.

We'd eat on the beach and spend a long time there lazing around.
I collected little shells.

Closer to the city, there was a wooden boardwalk.
From one side you could see the water or the sand down below.
On the other side were shops, games, merry-go-rounds, figure-8 roller
coasters, people selling cotton candy and nougat, and flea circuses.
The men would let the fleas run around on their arms, and the fleas fed
by biting them now and then.
It was funny.

You always ended up having to spend money on the boardwalk.
We didn't go there that often.

On the trip home, we'd stop and see a family we knew that lived halfway between Long Beach and Pasadena; they'd let us take a shower and change our clothes in their yard. They had an outdoor shower hooked up to their garage wall.

It made the return trip less unpleasant; my father didn't like sand itching him either.

My favorite excursions were on Sundays, when we'd drive along the base of the Sierra Madre foothills.

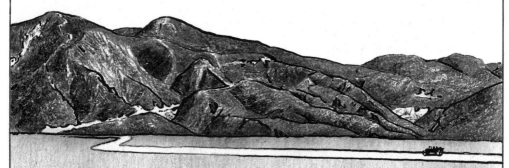

The foothills didn't have all that many trees, but there was lots of other vegetation; small streams flowed down from the mountain.

Sometimes we'd stop and pick wild gooseberries, and if my parents were in the mood, we'd walk around for a bit.

My Cope grandparents, when they came with us, tired quickly, and my parents didn't like the harder trails. But I loved them.

I wanted to keep climbing and go deeper into the scrubland.

I'd climb and climb, and my father would yell:

Don't go so far! We have to be able to see you!

I'd try to stay in sight while going as far as possible.

Later, as an adolescent, I sometimes went up into the mountains with friends.
Not often enough, though.
I was rarely able to take the afternoon off.
It's a shame.

I knew one trail that led deep into the foothills. You'd follow ravines or Arroyo Seco. It was a barely-marked trail that ran alongside streams and cut across them and back again.
There were yuccas everywhere.

In one spot I particularly liked, there was a deep pool of water enclosed in the depths of the rock face. We'd take our clothes off and go swimming.

The water was cold and crystal clear.

Farther along, we found ladders made of saplings. The rungs were old branches secured to the trunks with half-rotten ropes. I was light; I'd go up them. They looked as if they would fall apart at any minute, but they never did.

I arrived at a stand of huge trees; there were bay laurels, whose fragrance pervaded the whole area.

Higher up, nearer the open sky, the hot sun beat down on their leaves, bringing out the laurels' very distinctive scent, which really

permeates,

suffuses the air.

You had to watch out for poison ivy and know how to recognize it.
It looks like regular ivy, which trails on the ground and climbs trees.
If you touch it, it gives you a terrible rash that takes several days to heal,
even with applications of baking soda.

There were salamanders wandering around. Rattlesnakes, too. Lots of them.

ALAN, COME BACK HERE THIS MINUTE!

WE'RE GOING HOME!

I was never bitten, but I have an interesting story about a time when I nearly was.

ALAN!

I'll tell you about it later.

My father often took us to Mount Wilson Observatory, which is at
an altitude of about 6,000 feet. It made for a nice outing.
The mountains were beautiful, covered with tall pine trees.
The road was dangerous but passable.
They had put in little parking areas; oddly enough, given how wild
the area was, natural gas was piped in.
There were coin-operated heaters, but we rarely used them,
as they cost twenty-five cents.

Hanson

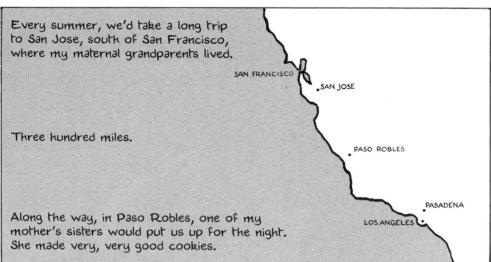

5

Every summer, we'd take a long trip
to San Jose, south of San Francisco,
where my maternal grandparents lived.

Three hundred miles.

Along the way, in Paso Robles, one of my
mother's sisters would put us up for the night.
She made very, very good cookies.

SAN FRANCISCO

SAN JOSE

PASO ROBLES

PASADENA

LOS ANGELES

The next day, we'd arrive at 340 North 12th Street, in San Jose.
It was a big one-story house, a very dark shade of brown,
not especially pretty. The foundation was solid sequoia.
Sequoia wood is rot-proof, fireproof, and termite-proof.

Outside there were street lamps left over
from the time when gas was used for lighting.
California had no shortage of natural gas.

Each of the main rooms of the house
had its own gas tap.
You turned it on by winding a small crank.

I used to do this thing: wearing
leather-soled shoes, I'd drag my feet
on the wool carpet in the living room
to build up static electricity.
Then I'd turn on the gas and touch the tap.
There'd be a spark, and then the gas,
which was very combustible, would go on.

I did that a lot.
Now that I think about it, it was probably pretty dangerous.

I've often regretted that I didn't know my grandfather
George Hanson better.
I knew him only as a very old man.
He died when he was ninety, when I was ten years old.
A considerable age.

He fought in the Civil War, for the North.
He was only sixteen, but he wanted to go to war so he lied about his age.
It was easy, he was big and tall.

Also, there was no real civil registry in the United States then;
each state did things its own way.
He left for the South with his unit, on foot.

They were stationed for a few days near a garden, where he met a very young girl. My grandfather got to know her over the fence. He told her:

"When the war is over,
I'll come back and make
you my wife."

And he did, but not right away.

After the war, he had to earn a living.
So he stayed in the army, like so many others did.
He fought in quite a few Indian wars.
Unfortunately, I wasn't able to get all that much out of his stories,
because I was too young and didn't really understand them.
I remember one in particular: he was a lookout patroling the
walkway of a fort somewhere in the desert, out west, on the plains.
It was dawn.

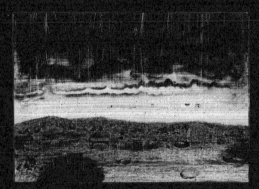

The fort was surrounded by bushes. All of a sudden my grandfather thought:

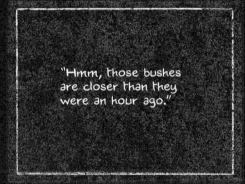

"Hmm, those bushes
are closer than they
were an hour ago."

The bushes were getting closer because each one had an Indian behind it.
So, that kind of anecdote.

Anyway, he came back to marry my grandmother.
It's a true story, just as simple as that.
Her maiden name was Lady Bayham,
a title that went back to the days
when her family had been English.
She was a nice person, not very educated,
who raised eight well-behaved children.

I can still see my grandfather sitting on the porch reading weekly magazines with stories about cowboys or the Civil War. I kept quite a few of them when he died, but as a teenager I didn't have the brains to save them. Those things had some great stories in them.

10 Cts.

THE BUFFALO BILL STORIES

A Weekly Publication devoted to Border History

He'd spread newspapers on the floor all around his rocking chair, so he could spit on them and not get the floor dirty.

STREET & SMITH
PUBLISHERS
NEW YORK

When he nodded off, I'd get some sticky paper, lick it, and glue it onto his head. He never said a word; he found it very funny.

I had a good voice and he'd ask me to sing some songs, but they were always Civil War songs that I didn't know.

What had his job been?
I had the sense he'd been in construction, but no one ever talked about it.

An outside stairwell led down into an enormous basement.

Inside was an unbelievable assortment of odd items,
random bits of hardware of all kinds—
nails, bolts, and bits and pieces of metal stored in cabinets.

There was also a hand-operated grindstone
for sharpening tools.
I'd play at turning the crank.
I must have been very young to find that entertaining.

I was told that all of that stuff had some connection
to my grandfather's old job; no further explanation was given.

Grandfather Hanson liked a big breakfast.
No corn flakes or anything like that.
They already existed, but he was against that sort of thing.
He wanted what he called real eating.

I remember those lavish breakfasts.
I didn't eat as much as he did, but I did eat plenty.
Breakfast was very early in the morning, around 6 o'clock.
You had to get up with the sun.
There were a lot of us at the big round table in the kitchen.

There was my Uncle Alton and his wife, Edith,
who lived with my grandparents.

Sometimes, other aunts and uncles and their families.

Me, my parents, and my grandparents.

That's a lot of people.

The coffee came from a percolator.
I drank chocolate milk, and my grandmother had tea.

There were sliced potatoes, pan-fried the way cowboys
make them, meaning you use raw potatoes, not cooked
ones. They were very good and were usually served
with ketchup, salt and pepper, and onions.

We poured milk and sugar on our oatmeal.
Grandfather added some butter.
With his knife, he'd carve out big chunks of butter,
place them at the four cardinal points of his bowl,
and watch them slide down and melt into his oatmeal.
I got into the habit of doing the same thing.

There was toast, of course.

Stewed fruit with a bit of sugar,
fresh peach halves, for instance.
If they weren't in season, my grandmother would get them from
jars she had put up with one or the other of her daughters-in-law.

Thick slices of fried ham.

A lot of boiled eggs, several per person, in a big salad bowl.

That would hold us until noon,
when we'd have a lighter meal.

In November 1930, when I was five, my grandparents invited the whole family to their golden anniversary celebration.
My father couldn't go because of his teaching job.
That was the one and only time that my mother and I went to San Jose by train.

We took the evening train from Glendale, near Los Angeles, like a lot of other people who wanted to avoid the big city.
It was the first stop after L.A., very close by.
In the old Hollywood movies,
people are always taking the train from Glendale,
a very photogenic little station.

We were in a Pullman car, a sleeping car. We had a compartment to ourselves.

A black conductor in an immaculate uniform converted our seats into beds, with nice white sheets and comfortable blankets.

In one corner was a small electric light, securely attached to the wall, that you could toggle on and off.

I still remember how happy I was to be sleeping in the same bed as my mother, turning the little night-light on and off and listening to the song of the steel wheels and rails.

I felt shy when we got to
my grandparents' house.
I didn't know all my aunts and uncles yet.
I had never met the majority of my
many cousins, most of whom
were older than me.
They never came to San Jose
in the summer.
Some of them lived in Sacramento,
quite a bit north of San Francisco.

I was a bit afraid of those big,
strapping boys.

The meal was a real event.
We were twenty-three people
at the dining room table.
A big sideboard separated us
from the kitchen.
Right in the middle of it was
a serving hatch with a sliding door.
The food was simple but delicious
and plentiful.

When the meat, mashed potatoes,
and vegetables went around for the
second time, everyone had already
eaten a lot.
I saw my cousins confer quickly,
and all of a sudden they announced
that they wanted seconds, but that
first they wanted to get some exercise.

We're going to run
around the block.

They got up
from the table.

The block was huge,
like they can be in California.
I had never been all the way
around it.
They left, shouting joyfully
and with abandon...

...and only came back after a long
while; their parents were starting
to worry.
Out of breath, they explained
that they had gone around twice,
given the state of their stomachs.

I was in a state of
inexpressible admiration.

They had second helpings as large as the first ones.
It's my favorite memory of that party.

Dessert, a huge white cake,
came through the kitchen door
just as the sun went down.
Each guest was given one of
the cake decorations: a little golden
bell. I kept mine for decades before
I eventually lost it.

If it's still around—and ringing—
somewhere, it must be ringing with
some of the happiness of that day.

We took some family photos in front of the house.
In this one, you can see my mother
and her four surviving brothers.
From left to right, Bill, Ed, George, and Alton.
My mother is twenty-eight years old.

Missing is an uncle I never knew, who died at forty-five of some disease.
That sort of thing used to happen a lot. Disease killed a lot of people.

Bill died in 1939.
He must have been the brother with whom my
father was play fighting, the day he met Bunny.

Ed and George died in '59.

Alton in '64.

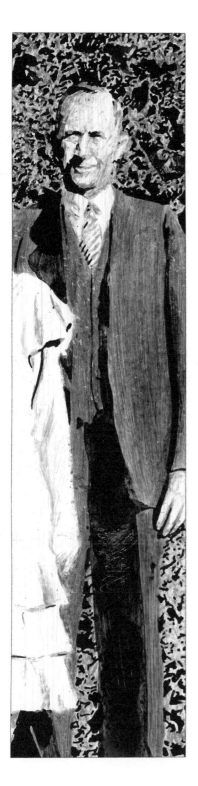

George and Alton worked for the railroad.
George was in goods transportation.
At the time, almost all freight
was transported by train, and George,
who was responsible for one of the routes
between San Francisco and Los Angeles,
made a very good living.
Much better than my father did
from teaching.
My mother liked George, and so did I.
He was nice.
He wrote us regularly, saying:
"If you want to meet me,
I'll be arriving on such and such a day
on the whatever o'clock train."

When my father was free,
we'd hop in our old car
and head over to the old Los Angeles
train station.

At that time, trains still ran on city roads. The tracks were right there on top of the pavement, like trolley tracks.

The train slowly pulling into the station made for an impressive sight. Automobile traffic halted to let the huge locomotive pass, its puffing punctuated by the clang! clang! clang! of its bell.

In those days, aerodynamics wasn't yet a factor in the design of land vehicles. Those locomotives were monuments— monsters.
To travel by train was to travel by black dragon. Locomotives would unexpectedly belch out jets of steam, startling you, and then, after gradually slowing down for what seemed an interminable period, come to a stop in a cloud of noise and smoke.

Uncle George, a giant,
would get out wearing his uniform.
He'd always say: "Hi, sonny!"
And give me a quarter.
Usually people gave me a penny
or five cents;
he never gave me less than
twenty-five cents.
We'd spend a little time together.
We'd talk.

Sometimes we'd watch him leave.
Railmen waved little flags at the
back of the train,
from the caboose, the last car.
In the evening and at night,
they held up oil lamps so that
the conductor could see them.
The stationmaster shouted:
"All aboard!"

I was allowed to run alongside the locomotive for
a little while, at a safe distance, so I could admire
the powerful pistons that drove the wheels, slowly,
slowly, and then faster and faster.

In those days, locomotives still had big, slatted, V-shaped
iron cowcatchers in front.
I was fascinated by them and wondered how they managed
to catch cows on the tracks when they hit them.
No one told me that the device was more for
the protection of the locomotive than of the cow.

When I drew a locomotive,
I always added on a really big cowcatcher.

Ed was the one who lived near Sacramento,
in the country.
The summer when I was eight,
we coaxed our old jalopy there,
just for a day and a night.
The house was very simple, prefabricated.
I think he had six kids, two girls and four boys.
They had a horse—
a working horse of my uncle's.
I can still see my young hosts
helping me learn to ride him bareback,
along a narrow path by the river.
It's a shame it was my only visit
and lasted such a short while.

Alton and his wife, Edith, married late
and had their only child,
my cousin Robert, at around forty.

In the late 1970s,
Aunt Edith lived alone
in my grandparents' house.
Everybody else had either died or left.
She sold it to move into a mobile home
in a retirement community in San Jose.
I got back in touch with her by letter in 1978.
She gave me all the details
that I'm providing here,
those that aren't personal memories.

This picture shows the whole family, except for the person who took it.

One of my aunts is also missing, my mother's favorite.
She'd been locked up for a few years in a mental institution.
Her story was a tragedy for the whole family.

She'd married a man who was nice but fairly worthless. He gambled and drank.

During Prohibition, he'd go out drinking in clubs in San Francisco's Chinatown, which wasn't far from their house.

She loved her husband and would go fetch him home from those underground clubs, where people drank anything and everything.

She'd drag him home, practically carrying him.

One thing led to another, and she, too, started to drink.

Because it was Prohibition, the alcohol was bad, and she lost her mind; her husband, who was tougher, didn't.

He's the one who had her committed to the asylum where she remained until she died, at around age fifty.

My mother spoke of her often, because she was a very good person, the most stylish of all the sisters, always well dressed, who knew a thing or two about art.

One day, when I was about ten, I received a very pretty handmade Valentine's Day card from her. That was the only contact I ever had with her.

In a moment of lucidity, she had thought about her nephew.

The man with the wavy hair is Uncle Dick,
a German immigrant.
As a young man, he lost everything
in the San Francisco earthquake, in 1906,
except his life, his pajamas, and his canary.
He owned a small restaurant
and lent my father money
so that he could finish college
in Santa Barbara.

Standing next to him is his wife,
my Aunt Emma.
She died five years later
of stomach cancer.
A Christian Scientist,
she refused medical care.

Behind Emma, the lady with the round face
is my Paso Robles aunt,
who made such good cookies.

I'm the little boy standing to the right.

I said earlier that I was very impressed
by my older cousins. That day, however,
I began a friendship with the boy with
curly hair whose soles are completely
visible in the picture. I liked him a lot.

At the end of the day,
when almost everyone else
had gone home,
my grandmother said to me;
"You got along well with your cousin.
He's nice, isn't he?" She was happy that
I had gotten close to at least one of them.

It's true, I would have liked
to be friends with him.

I never saw that cousin again,
and I'm certain that I never thought of him
even once in the past sixty years.

It's the fact that I'm diving down deep
to tell you this story,
far beneath my conscious memory
that brought it back to me
on the night of November 9 to 10, 1996.

In the middle, my grandparents, George and Mary Emma Hanson.
Four or five years later, we got word that my grandfather was dying,
so my father, my mother, and I went up to San Francisco.
When we got there, we saw his body being carried out of his bedroom.
He was covered with a sheet, but only the top part of him.
I was still quite small and I'm sure that I'm the only one who saw
something that really surprised me: the extraordinary length of his testicles,
which were hanging down.

As a Civil War veteran (there were hardly any left by then)
He was entitled to military honors.
Eight uniformed soldiers, rifles on their shoulders, formed an
honor guard outside the funeral home.
None of the funerals I'd been to as a small child
Had included such a protocol; I was impressed.

I'll tell you some more about my grandmother
Hanson when I talk about my adolescence.

Cope

6

My grandfather Cope was an admirable man, a lathe operator,
but his life was a bit less—how shall I say?—
colorful.
He liked simplicity.

His name was Hilburn M. Cope;
he never knew for sure what the "M" stood for.
He was from a small pottery town in North Carolina.
His father worked in real estate.
Soon the family moved to Pennsylvania.

That's where my grandfather met my grandmother.

Her name was Ione Ingram, of Anglo-Saxon descent.
She was the youngest of five children.
She had four brothers who were quite far apart in age.
Her father had wanted only sons, so he gave her a boy's name:
Ione instead of Iona.
Ione is a very pretty name.

Even she admitted that as a child she'd been very spoiled by her four brothers.
Well, spoiled—she had no money, she was as poor as a church mouse,
but her brothers loved her and indulged her.
Her favorite was the youngest, Howard,
who made excellent pancakes outdoors, on a piece
of soapstone.
(Soapstone is an oily-looking stone;
you can light a fire underneath and the pancake won't stick to it.)

All four brothers died fairly young, of various illnesses.

Their father's name was Jim,
but people called him "Whittling Jim."

He was a very hard-working man.
He built his own home out of stone
and lived a completely self-sufficient life with
his family. He raised horses, cows, and pigs,
grew grain crops and fruit trees.
He smoked his own hams.
His wife did the spinning and weaving.
We used to have one of her tablecloths.
It covered a pretty round living room table
that Whittling Jim had carved out of wood
from one of his many cherry trees.
When he chopped down one of those trees,
he'd cut it up into boards and make furniture,
always by hand, or smaller items.

I still have a cherry wood writing box
I inherited from my grandmother
that has a penholder with 24-carat gold trim,
a gold ball at the end, and a gold nib.
I can show you the box, but not the
penholder, which I gave away one day under
circumstances I'll tell you about later.

Our family memorabilia included
a daguerreotypeof the farm
that Whittling Jim built.
It was a simple two-story house
overlooking a field.
I used to look at that daguerreotype
a lot when I was little.

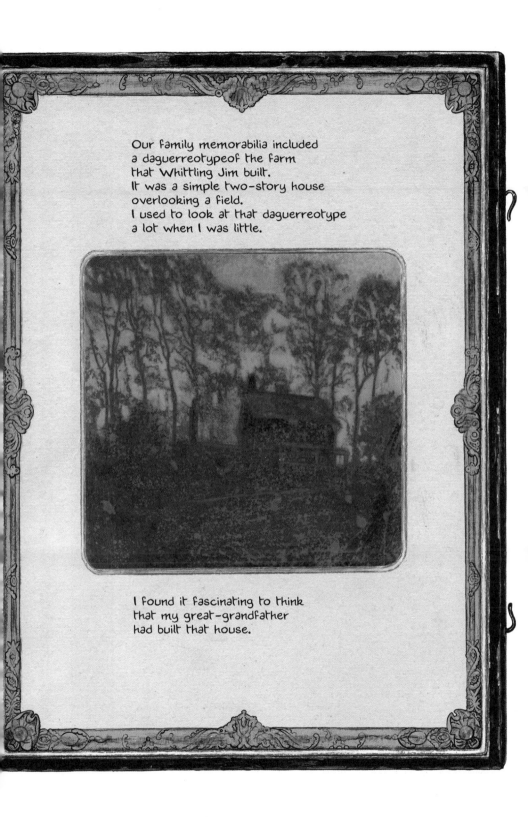

I found it fascinating to think
that my great-grandfather
had built that house.

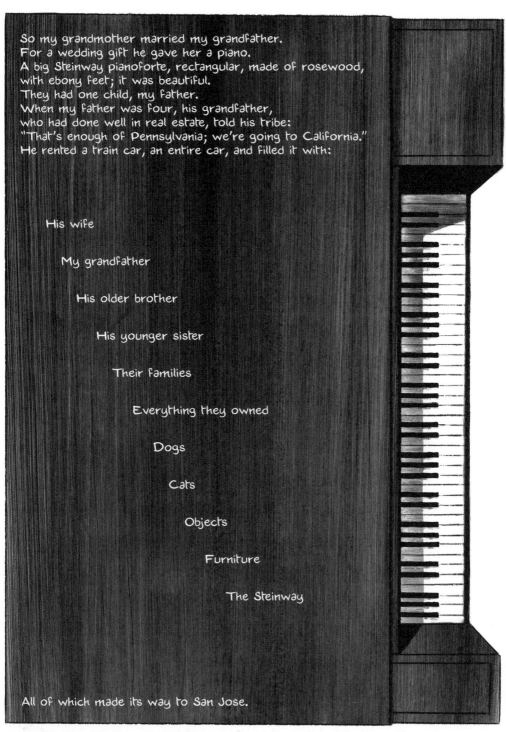

So my grandmother married my grandfather.
For a wedding gift he gave her a piano.
A big Steinway pianoforte, rectangular, made of rosewood,
with ebony feet; it was beautiful.
They had one child, my father.
When my father was four, his grandfather,
who had done well in real estate, told his tribe:
"That's enough of Pennsylvania; we're going to California."
He rented a train car, an entire car, and filled it with:

His wife

My grandfather

His older brother

His younger sister

Their families

Everything they owned

Dogs

Cats

Objects

Furniture

The Steinway

All of which made its way to San Jose.

And that's why I'm a Californian.

One of my Cope grandmother's stories:

When your father was a child, the whole family liked to go camping in the forests north of San Francisco.
We had big, heavy tents and slept on canvas beds.

One night, I was sleeping on my back and all of a sudden I felt short of breath. My chest felt like it was being crushed; I was suffocating.

I opened my eyes. A dark shape was leaning over me; I could feel its breath.

It was a bear's head.

A bear?

A huge bear who was sniffing my face.

His paws were on my chest. I was terrified.

Did you scream?

No, luckily.

The fear and the weight of the bear made it hard to breathe.

What did you do?

Nothing. There was nothing I could do.

He left. I woke your grandfather, who was sleeping like a log.

Later, I realized why the bear was sniffing me like that.

Why?

We had eaten bacon and eggs that night, so I probably smelled like bacon.

He probably thought: "Wow, this woman sure smells good."

You were lucky.

The old patriarch of the Copes moved his real estate business
from San Francisco to Los Angeles.
When he died, he left his two sons two beautiful wood houses on one lot,
in the city of Alhambra. So the families moved to Southern California.

I don't know why, but on my
grandfather's house there was a
mortgage held by his older brother,
Linford.

The two brothers didn't like each other.
Their wives didn't either.
Linford had been strange since
the death of his first wife;
he'd turned nasty.
His second wife was strange, too.

When the Great Depression of 1929 hit, my grandfather lost his job and could
no longer make his monthly payments to Linford. There was a foreclosure.
Linford took the house back and threw my grandparents out.

It ruined their old age.

My grandfather had more and
more trouble finding work,
and they often had to come
live with us.

That's when his duodenal
ulcer got worse.

My grandmother was a hypochondriac,
always imagining she had one illness or another;
she was charming, though.
I loved her very much,
and I have only good memories of her.

So of course there was no question of ever seeing mean old Uncle Linford.

I'll skip a few years.
When I was nineteen, right before I went to war in Europe, I thought:

I have to meet my great-uncle.
Everyone hates him, but after all, he's my
great-uncle. Why did he do what he did?
I'd like to know.

I told my grandparents:

I'm going to see Uncle Lin!

They didn't object.

We understand.

I showed up at his house
in uniform.

I found a stone-deaf old man.
He and his wife welcomed me warmly.
He generally stayed put in one room
and didn't get around much.
Around his neck he had a slate
with a piece of chalk,
so he could communicate.

He hadn't always been that way.
When he was still active, he'd been a very good zinc worker
who made a lot of money building huge fans, turbine ventilators for factories,
that sort of thing.
On top of that, like his father, he had been successful in real estate.
So they had everything they could possibly want.

We couldn't really talk because of his condition.
At one point he handed me two watches.

Here. They're
for you.

107

One was gold, the other antique silver. Two wonderful items that worked perfectly and that you had to wind with a key.

He showed me that the silver one had a crystal that was specially ground in the center.
You could open it up, put it in front of a keyhole, and if the keyhole wasn't too deep, you could see everything that was going on in the room.

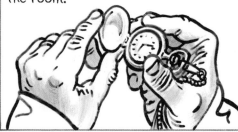

I'm giving them to you, and you're going to sell them.

No, never.

Yes, you will. You'll see. One day you'll be broke and you'll sell them.

The gold watch made it through the Second World War in my fatigues pocket. God knows I got banged up and knocked around a lot, but it never broke.

Years later, in France, when I was married and the father of three children, I had to sell both watches because I had run out of money.

To my great regret, I had fulfilled Uncle Lin's prophecy.

When I left, his wife said to me:

Come with me, I want to show you something.

I followed her up to the attic.

She took me over to a huge wardrobe with lots of shelves, like in a library. On the shelves were hundreds and hundreds of small hardcover notebooks.

Look.

What is all this?

It's his whole life, from the age of twenty on. No one from your side of the family has ever seen this.

On the pages of those small notebooks, every penny of his daily income and expenses was recorded.

This notebook, for instance, was for a short trip I took without him.

I had to record all my expenses during that trip, including the cost of the stamp for the letter I had to send him every day, so that he could keep the books from a distance.

Everything was there:

Bread, butter, milk, potatoes, gas, clothing... every day for more than fifty years.

I saw it with my own eyes.

That's when I understood that my uncle had a psychological illness and that it would have been absolutely impossible, with that kind of mentality, for him to have extended to his brother even the most minimal amount of credit.

But he did give me the two watches.

I'm showing you this so that you'll know who your great-uncle is. And also because you came to see us.

My great-aunt looked like a woman who'd been caught in a trap and who'd accepted her fate.

I didn't tell my grandfather or my grandmother the story of the notebooks.
We were very open with each other, but I just didn't dare.
I left for the war, and while I was gone, they both died in poverty and in sorrow.

I'll go back to my younger days.
After Uncle Lin threw them out,
my grandparents frequently had to come live with us,
which meant that we had to rent larger houses
so that they could have their own room.
I have to say that this arrangement suited me.
My grandmother was the kind of woman
to be jealous of her son,
but she got along well with my mother.
I can still see her munching on an apple.

Here's a picture of her:

You can see clearly that,
as a young bride,
she had been very pretty.
She was a small woman,
while my grandfather was
very tall and very thin.

He was handsome, too.

7

Under the first house they moved into with us, there was a big crawl space.
It was...maybe not quite three feet, but at least thirty inches high.
I was six, and it was easy for me to squeeze into.

During the summer season, which lasts quite a long time in California, I used to get up early, before the rest of the household.

I'd get dressed, which I had learned to do by myself, and go into to the kitchen, where I'd get a jar with a lid.

I'd go out of the house and slip into the crawl space through a little wooden door, which I'd leave open, to let in some light.

Air vents in the side panels also let some light in.

I could see well enough to catch spiders.

There were all kinds of them, but my favorites were the black widows.
I liked their round bellies, like marbles, with a red spot on the Mrs.
The Mrs. eats the Mr. after they mate.

I'd hold a jar in my left hand, its lid in my right hand and

CLICK!

I'd trap them.

My parents hated that pastime, especially since black widows are very dangerous.
Their bite can kill a little boy if not treated immediately.

They'd destroy my spiders, forbid me to catch them, and I'd do it again.

It was when we lived in that house that I learned the word

KLEENEX

I'd always used cloth handkerchiefs.

We started seeing ads in magazines showing a well-dressed, healthy-looking little girl with golden curls. I could read a bit. The ad said: "Oh, she's so pretty! She's so healthy! She uses Kleenex!"

I had no idea what a Kleenex might be.

I found out one day that a little girl who lived up the street had a box of Kleenex. That's how I met her. She was pretty nice, and sometimes we'd play together.

I wonder what happened to her.

No idea.

Another first was the time I went to the movies one day
with my parents and my grandparents.
It wasn't the first movie I'd seen, far from it.
We lived near Hollywood, and there were movies all over the place.
This one was called "The House of Rothschild."

It was in black and white, like all movies, but all of a sudden everyone went "Oh!"

No one had ever seen a color film before; it was the very beginning.

I was very interested in dragons when I was little.
I drew them and collected pictures of them.

On Colorado Boulevard,
Pasadena's main street,
there was a Chinese shop owner,
a nice older man
who sold all sorts of Chinese items
and products,
from very cheap to quite expensive.

My grandmother,
who didn't have much money,
liked to spoil me and every so often
would take me to the Chinese man
to buy me some small thing.
Small, but Chinese.

For not a lot of money you could buy
those wonderful paper flowers
that bloom in a bowl of water,
or some candied ginger.

Once she went for broke
and bought me a little box
I had often admired
but which somehow had never sold.
It was made of black lacquer, with
an inlaid dragon in mother of pearl.
I think the owner gave her
a good price.

I kept it safe until I left for the war.
It probably got broken.

That dragon was one of things
I really loved.

My grandparents had gone to live elsewhere, but right as we were about to move, they were preparing to come back.

So we rented another house.
It was quite large, fairly old,
and the rent was cheap.
It was on a street corner in Altadena.
The street was lined with olive trees.

When the weather got warm,
miracle of miracles,
berries appeared on the trees.

When the olives were ripe,
I climbed one of the trees
and picked some nice black ones
and stuck them in my mouth.

If you've never tried that, do.

I screamed, spat them out,
and ran home.
The mucous membranes in
my mouth started to swell,
and kept on swelling.
It was unbelievable.
The taste was awful.

I explained what had happened to me as best I could.
That's when they explained to me that olives have to be cured
for a long time in lye and salt before you can eat them.
No one had warned me.
Adults always think that children know things that they really don't.

Our neighbors were just like us.
The grandparents lived with them,
for all the same reasons.
They came from some backwater
and made their own soap.
They shared it with us.

They kept a goat, which I learned how to milk.
I liked milking it, and I liked its milk.

118

I remember very clearly that when we were living
there, there was a big earthquake whose epicenter
was in Long Beach, about thirty miles from us.

Long Beach felt a strong jolt; there was a tidal wave.
All the school buildings crumbled.
Barely a half hour had elapsed
since the end of the school day.
People realized what a disaster it would have been if
the earthquake had struck during school hours.

It was at that point that it became mandatory
to make schools earthquake-proof
by using new construction techniques
and organizing regular
safety drills.

My grandmother's Steinway pianoforte, her wedding gift, was at our house.
It started to play all by itself because of the vibrations of the earthquake.
After the shaking stopped, the ground vibrated softly for a long time.
You could hardly feel it, but the piano captured the vibrations, which traveled
up its legs. The strings kept on producing sounds.
My grandmother and my mother were afraid.
They told my father: "Well, do something! You have to make it stop!"
We tried, we put things on top of it, but the piano wouldn't be silent.
It vibrated for hours and hours.

That piano followed my grandmother wherever she went.
She didn't play well, but she did play and she enjoyed it.
It had a beautiful sound.
I learned how to play on it. Later, it was taken from me.
That was one of the tragedies of my life.

We left the house with the olive trees for Navarro Avenue, west of Pasadena.

I was a bit older, nine or so.

I was allowed to roller skate in the neighborhood and even beyond.
My grandparents moved again, a few miles away, and I'd go see them.

The sidewalks were amazing;
they were smooth, downhill cement slopes.

I'd come home on the intercity streetcar.

North of Navarro Avenue, in the base of the foothills, lived a boy around my age.

To me it seemed as if his house and yard were suspended at a tremendous height.

Probably for that reason, he thought of himself as the king of the mountain.

He refused to let me through when I wanted to go up there to explore.

Go away! It's my sidewalk! It's my street!

I'll punch you and kill you if go any farther!

I was pretty timid, I have to say. I didn't dare confront him.

My father made fun of me.

Alan, you're ridiculous. All you have to do is punch him in the nose, hard. You'll see, he'll start crying.

Maybe.

But that wasn't my style, so I left him to yell all by himself on top of his mountain.

I think that one time I managed to get through because he wasn't there. On my way back down, he saw me and yelled at me:

Get out of here!

One day, on my way home from school, I ran into him on a street corner.

Because we were level, I realized he was small and skinny.

He started in on me again.

You wanna fight?

So? You wanna fight?

No.

So I punched him in the nose, not too hard. But I'd had enough.

That was about my only fight as a child.

Waah!

I'm going to tell my mother!

So that's the story of the king of the mountain.

When we lived on Navarro Avenue, I had a big female duck, as big as a goose.
Her name was Ebb.
It's a boy's name, but we had thought she was a male duck.
And then she started to lay eggs.

She was mute,
the kind of Chinese duck that
doesn't go quack-quack.

She ran loose in the yard.
She'd hunt for wood lice under
rocks and on the edges of
flower beds.

When it rained,
the water would
rush through the
gutters at top
speed.

Ebb would come
out of the yard.

She'd get herself
comfortable in
the gutter and
float down to
the bottom of
the street.

She'd come back
up on foot, on
the sidewalk, and
do it all over
again.

As long as there
was enough
water, she'd keep
doing it. She
really loved it.

Sometimes I'd bring her to school.
We'd put her on the lawn and the students would play with her.

Was it to imitate my duck?
I had a little metal wagon, the kind they used to make. Four wheels.
I'd get in it, grab the handle to steer, give a kick, and head on down
my street.

It worked pretty well, but I wasn't satisfied.

I found a large wooden panel, which I put on top of the wagon.

On top of that, I balanced a little table and chair I had taken from my room.

On the table, I put some paper and a pencil.

I couldn't pull the handle back toward me, so I left it out in front
and tied a rope to it.

I'd push off and try to write or draw on my little table as the wagon rolled along.

I steered by pulling on the rope and lifting the handle so that it wouldn't drag on the ground.

There was no one on the sidewalk; it was a residential area.

When I got to the bottom, I'd leap off and bring everything to a stop.

It rarely toppled over.
I usually managed to make it work.

I had that kind of craziness.

The most common tree in the neighborhood was a
kind of camphor laurel.
It produced odd-looking seed pods.
Five pods spread out from the stem in a star shape,
each one filled with seeds.

The pods would drop onto the ground, and I'd pick them up.

I had learned in a magazine how to make birds out of them.

First I'd take off four of the five pods.
I'd remove the seeds from the fifth one and fill it with cotton.
That became the body.

The part that connected the pods to the central stem became the head and neck. The beak was the sharpened stem.

With pipe cleaners, I'd make legs for the bird and glue them onto a small piece of wood from a fig tree.

Then I'd look for some feathers to cover it with.
My grandmother had the idea to take me to some hatmaker shops.
At the time, the world's birds weren't protected, and you could get the most sumptuous feathers from exotic birds.
Hatmakers used them to decorate women's hats.
They had a lot left over and were happy to give me some.

I'd fit the back part of the pod with part of a feather, which became the tail.

Then I'd glue some feathers onto the sides, which became the wings.

And behind the head, one that formed a crest.

It took a long time, and I took great care. My birds were very pretty.

During one of my Sunday afternoon walks with my grandparents,
we'd sometimes stop in to see two women,
two not-so-young sisters who had a beautiful house in an orange grove.
They made candied orange, lemon, and grapefruit peel.
It's a very labor-intensive process, and even then that kind of candy was
expensive.

When you peel the fruit, you have to be careful to avoid the white part.
You cut the peel into strips about a quarter-inch wide.
Those you dunk several times in boiling water and then press them flat,
to get rid of the bitterness while retaining the fragrance.
You spread them on a rack and sprinkle them with powdered sugar
and let them bake in the sun, under some cheesecloth netting, for weeks.
The cheesecloth, of course, is to protect them from the clouds of insects
wanting to get at them.
Every night you have to bring the racks back inside,
and you can't put them out on cloudy days.
When the peels are properly candied, you add raw sugar and preserve them
in glass jars.
They're delicious.

One day, my grandmother told those ladies: "My grandson makes birds."
After that, every time we went there I'd bring some along.
They sold them to the customers who bought their candy.
The next time, they'd give me the money.
They'd always say: "You can make a lot more."
But bit by bit I got busy with my studies
and I stopped making the birds.

Still on Navarro, on the other side of the avenue, a bit farther down, lived a family whose father was a pastor.

There was the mother, a few almost-adult children, and a girl my age called Ruthy, or Ruth.

For me, the father was a bit of an enigma.
I didn't like him one bit.
A cold, severe man.
His church was more than twelve miles away.
I used to wonder why he lived so far from his church.
In my child's mind, I suspected that his congregation didn't like him, and that he wanted to live apart from them so people wouldn't bother him.

I really have no idea.

The family was very poor.
They rented a wood house of a decent size.

The floors were cheap pine.

Not one rug.

Not one extra chair.

Not one extra table.

The absolute minimum of furniture.

No couch where you could get comfortable.

They ate poorly.

I didn't like the father, but Ruthy was nice. I had a lot of fun with her. My parents and grandparents thought she was very ugly, and maybe she was.

I thought she looked all right.

There was a lot of land behind their house. No yard, more like a wasteland.

We'd climb up onto the flat roof of the garage, using the ladder that stood there.
The roof was shaded by the branches of a huge tree.
The first branch was so high up, we couldn't even touch it.

That was our playground.

We played all sorts of games,
the way children do.
We even tried to put on a play,
but we couldn't find anyone
to do it with us.
I'd pinned up some fabric and made a
fairly ridiculous-looking curtain.

My whole childhood,
I kept trying to put on a play,
but I never managed to.

Their house had an attic.
None of the worthless junk piled up in there had any value.

The only really interesting thing was a kind of music box
about the size of an old-fashioned record player,
with a handle and a metallic plate,
but no speaker, arm, or needle.
You'd put in a huge steel disc.
The pins on the revolving disc plucked bronze teeth
just like the ones in harmoniums.
We'd turn the handle very slowly and listen to the music;
we did that maybe hundreds of times.
There were three or four different discs in a box.

A fascinating item.

Later, I was forbidden to see that
little girl again. I obeyed.

When I was about fourteen, I was
out roller skating, and I ran into her,
quite a distance from the house.
We were happy to see each other.
I realized she'd become quite a
young woman, with a fairly nice body.
Probably just as ugly,
but I still couldn't see it.

So that's Ruthy.

You remember that I mentioned a story about a rattlesnake?

There were a lot of them in California. In the mountains, for instance. I said earlier that you could hear them.

They shake the little rattles at the end of their tails. It makes a fair amount of noise, LUCKILY. You HAVE to be able to hear them.

If you can hear them, it's not too dangerous; just don't go toward the sound.

But if you're right nearby and they don't hear you coming, then they have no choice but to bite you.

That's why, when you hike in wilderness areas, it's best to talk loudly, sing, do anything at all to make sure that they can hear you coming from far away.

I was ten or eleven.
My parents and I had been invited
to visit a couple that they knew, in
their cabin at the edge of the desert.
It was completely isolated, in very,
very wild country.

The cabin had oil lamps,
well water, and cooking facilities.

We spent Saturday night there,
and Sunday morning we got up
before dawn to hunt rabbits.

The mothers stayed home.
Both fathers, the couple's daughter,
and I left and walked for
a long time.

We walked single file.
My father was last, and I was next-to-last.

My father had his .22 long rifle. He wasn't a hunter, it wasn't really his thing, but he liked target shooting.

All of a sudden I felt a rush of air by my right foot and, at the same time, I realized that my father had fired a shot.

I'd just walked right past a big rattlesnake, a diamondback, who'd raised his head to strike at my ankle.

My father saw him.

No time to aim by sight. It was all or nothing, and he shot from the hip.

His aim was so good that the .22-caliber bullet went right through the snake's head without damaging its beautiful skin.

You have to cut the head off and bury it deep because the poison is still in the fangs.

We cut its head off, dug a hole and buried it, and then the daughter and I carried the snake.

I had the front part. Blood was dripping from it.
It was a bit more than five feet long, not too bad.
Just for comparison, I'm five foot nine.

It was a pretty impressive thing.

We headed back toward the cabin.
The mothers watched us approach.
From far away they caught sight of
the snake, which was still twitching.
They were terrified.

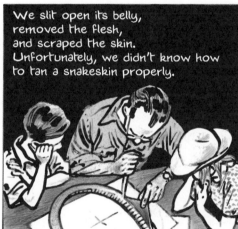

We slit open its belly,
removed the flesh,
and scraped the skin.
Unfortunately, we didn't know how
to tan a snakeskin properly.

Once we got home, we put it on a board, and it decorated my room.

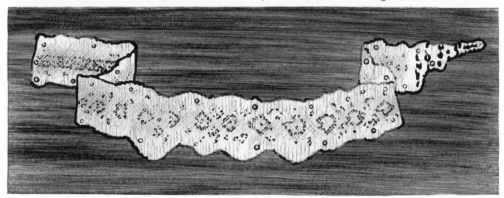

It was pretty, but since it hadn't been tanned, it ended up decomposing.

What's much more interesting than the snake, maybe,
is that later in the day we all took a walk together.

We went up into the hills, where there were old Indian adobe
cave dwellings.

The rooms were carved vertically out of the rock, and the wooden ladders
used to access them were still there.

I actually saw that.
It impressed me a lot more than the snake had because I liked it.

8

One day in late 1936, my mother said to me:

Alan, I'm going to have an operation.

She explained to me that when I was born, the doctor hadn't done a good job. She'd given birth in an awful little house that he rented to deliver babies in— a solution for people who had very little money to spend on medical expenses.

Maybe if my mother had given birth at home, things would have gone better.

In any case, she'd had trouble with her sex life ever since.
That doesn't mean she didn't have one, but it caused her increasing pain.
She and my father had decided that it was time for her to have her prolapsed organs removed, so that she could have a more pleasant and more normal life.

It's a surgical operation that today is referred to as a "total."

I was used to the more or less continual
presence of my parents.
Dad worked, Mom stayed home.
I was shy, somewhat sickly,
and my parents were worried
about the effect that my
mother's being gone
for at least a week
would have on me.

(My grandparents weren't living with
us at the time.)

The daughter of one of my father's
fellow teachers was called Caroline.
She was eighteen and in her senior year.
Like almost everyone else at the time,
she was looking to earn some money.

That fellow teacher suggested to my
father that Caroline come to the house
in the evenings to take care of us in my
mother's absence.

My parents agreed.

My mother explained everything to me.
I didn't show much fear or disapproval.

One December morning, I was playing ball in the street.
I can still see it as if it were yesterday.

My father and mother drove out of the yard.
They pulled up next to me.

My mother was in the passenger's seat; she rolled her window down.

I'm sorry to leave you like this.
Be good. Do what your father says.

Caroline will be coming by in
the evening to make dinner,
every day until I come back.
Understand? I'll be back
in a week.

Then something really terrible happened to me.
I was seized by a kind of panic.
I hadn't really understood that I would be without my mother for that long.
I don't know what went through my head, but I got angry.

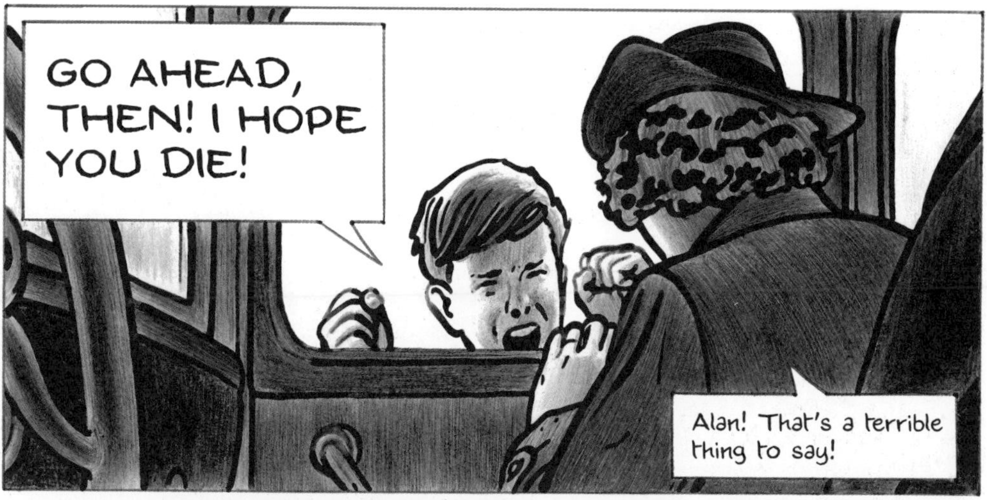
GO AHEAD, THEN! I HOPE YOU DIE!
Alan! That's a terrible thing to say!

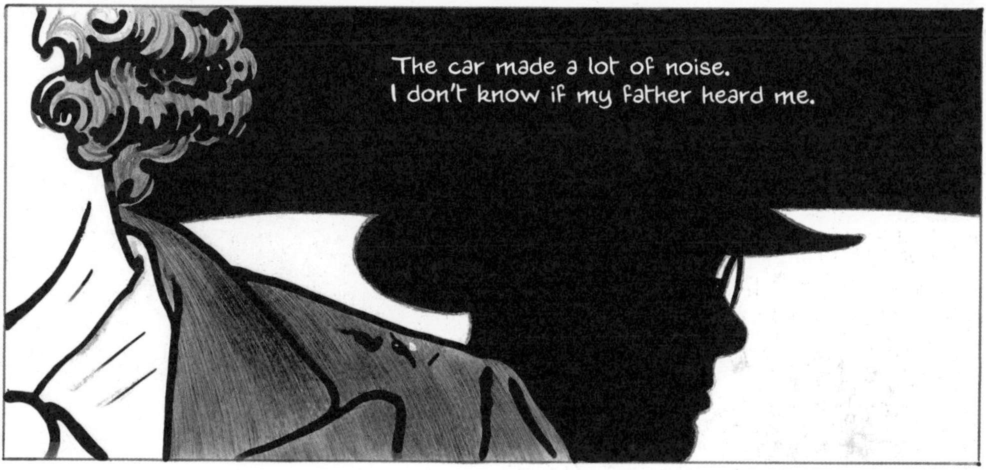
The car made a lot of noise.
I don't know if my father heard me.

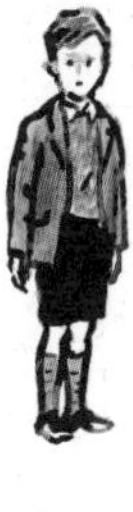

They left.

Caroline came by that night to make dinner.

It was December; it had been dark for a while.
My father, Caroline, and I were supposed to go see a movie.
Probably to take my mind off things that first night.
The idea of a movie was a real thrill for me.
Dinner was ready, and Caroline was getting worried about my father.

It got later and later.

Finally my father arrived.
His breath was hot in the cold air and
steam was coming out of his mouth.
His face was haggard,
tear-stained.

His first words were:

Well, my boy, we're going to have to learn how to fend for ourselves.

That was his way of telling me that my mother was dead.

I thought I understood, but he still had to spell it out for me.

Caroline was devastated.

I remembered
what I'd said that morning,
and it was very painful.
To this day,
I regret having said that.
I don't know if my father
heard me; I hope not.
We never spoke of it.

Later, I heard that my mother
had woken up after the operation.
I wonder if she thought
about what I'd said.
She couldn't not have,
but she knew me;
we adored each other.
She couldn't possibly have thought
that I was speaking from the heart,
that I really knew what I was saying,
or that some kind of fate existed on which
I'd had a sort of fantastical effect.

That said, I would have preferred if
it hadn't happened.

So it was a very unpleasant evening.
I remember that I didn't fully accept what had happened.
I kept asking Caroline:

So are we still going
to the movies?

That enraged her.
She didn't understand
how I could ask such a
question.
Me, I understand it
very well.
I was obviously trying
to deny reality.

The news spread quickly through the neighborhood.
The neighbors started to arrive.

They must have thought that they had the duty to be pleasant, to be good
neighbors, to express their condolences, and to stay awhile, for a sort of wake.

It was very upsetting.

We didn't have a phone, and neither did my grandparents.
They only showed up the next day.

The living room was full of people.
Almost all of them sitting down, either in silence or talking quietly
to one another.
Someone went to get the pastor, Ruthy's father.
He arrived and said:

Let us pray.

We all bowed our heads.
He said a very long prayer.
Protestants make up their prayers as they go along;
they don't have any ready-made.

At first I wasn't so pleased that he'd done that,
but what he said wasn't too bad.
I was pretty satisfied and surprised, too.

Later, everyone left, and that was the beginning of my life without my mother.

I didn't shed a tear,
although I was terribly sad and usually I
cried easily, out of habit. Not a tear.

I thought: "It's horrible, I don't have
a mother anymore. These things can
happen in life."

I'd heard of such things, of course,
children who lost their mothers.
Two friends of mine lived nearby in a
house; an old lady took care of them.
She wasn't even related to them;
she worked for social services.
They were dreadfully poor, and people
would say to me: "They're orphans—
their parents are dead."
I had understood that such a thing could
happen, but I never thought it could
happen to me, any more than I could
imagine losing a leg in an accident.

So I thought:
"If that's the way it is, that's the way
it is. I have to live with it."

I had the feeling that I had come across
a vast, important, earth-shattering
experience that was much too sad for
me to cry about.

Something big that showed me,
all of a sudden, how the world was.

I was kept at home for two days, so I wouldn't break down at school.
I wouldn't have broken down.

When I went back, everybody knew.

My father had told my teacher, and she had told my classmates.

They were pretty nice to me,
I have to say.
But the fact that I was getting
special treatment made me think.
I was like that, always thinking.

So I thought: "I've become important because an important thing
happened to me. It's embarrassing, and I think it's silly.
They should treat me like they usually do."

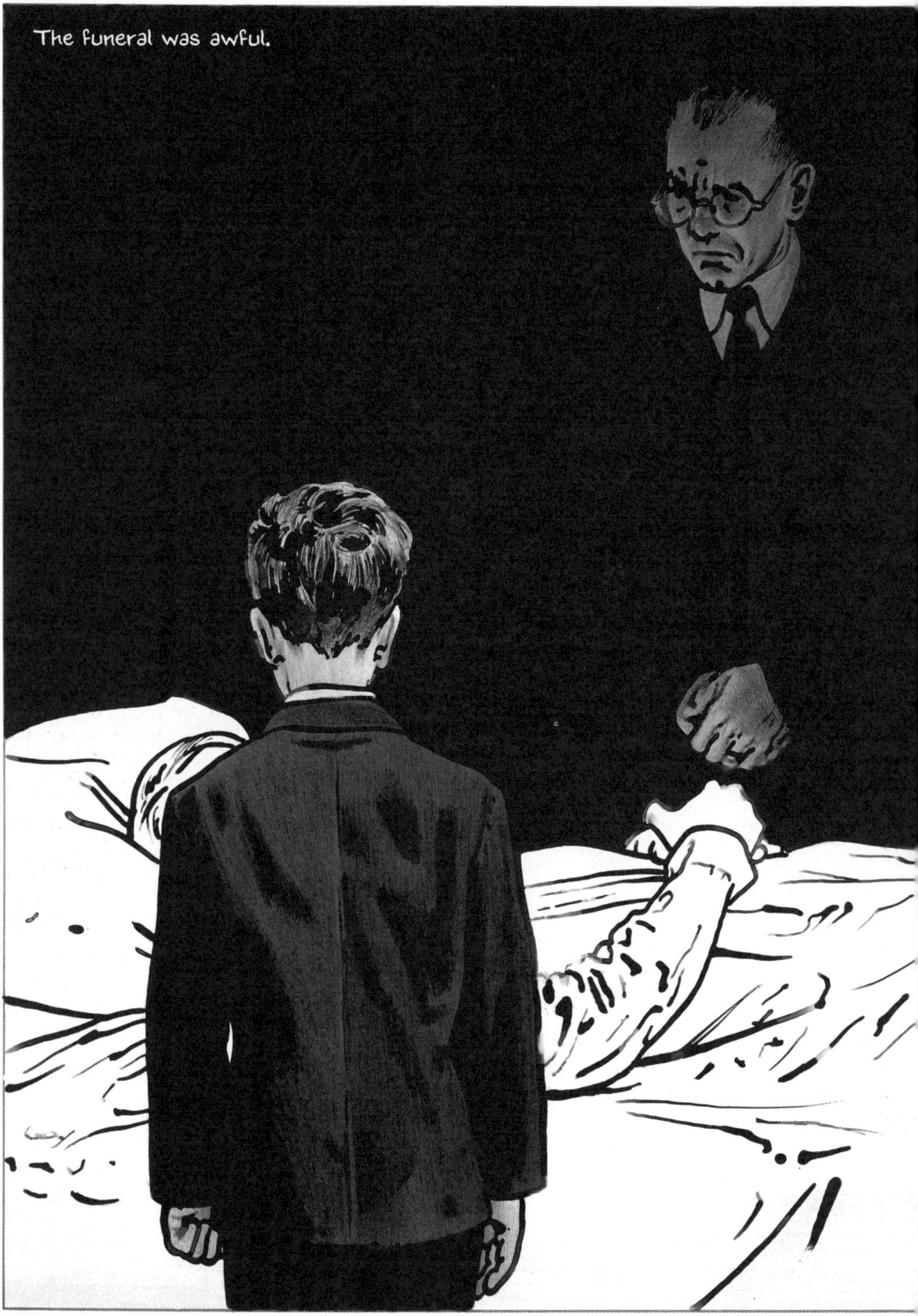
The funeral was awful.

My mother was laid out in a room that looked like a bedroom,
with a small nightstand and a nice bed.
They kept her there for a week.

Family members from up north, her mother,
some of her brothers, her sisters-in-law all came.
There were a lot of people.

They took me to see her several times.
They told me to kiss her.
I kissed her.
She didn't smell bad at all.
They'd made her up.
She looked like she was still alive.

I don't like that way of dealing with the dead.
It upset me and made me sad.
That's all I can say.
I knew full well that this person
who had been dead for a week had been my mother,
but I had trouble seeing why I was being
made to do this.

I preferred my memories of her; I had enough of them.

I attended Sunday school, as I mentioned earlier.
My parents had stopped going to church, but I still went.
I liked it there, I had friends.
We sang nice hymns and talked about this and that.

When I was younger, at an age when I could still believe such things,
it had been explained to me that when a mother died,
she became a star in the sky.
In California there are a lot of stars, especially in the desert.

I'd also been taught to say my prayers before going to sleep.
Most of the time I didn't, though.

I didn't believe in the star story, but I started to have long, long
conversations with my mother, at night, kind of like prayers.

I'd tell her what had happened to me that day,
the problems I'd had, and even about the good things.
I'd ask her questions, ask for her advice.

I didn't claim to receive any answers.
I'd say to her: "Guide me," as if I were talking to God.
I did that for a long time.

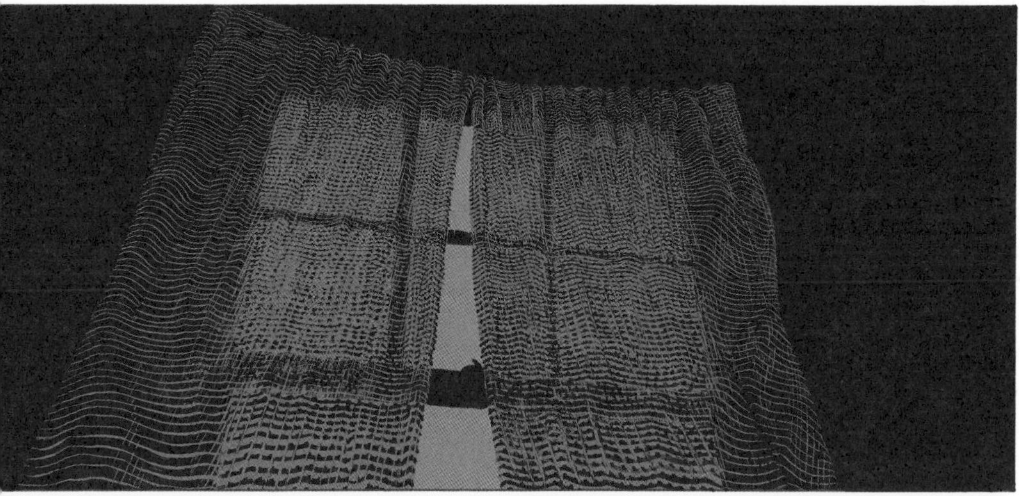

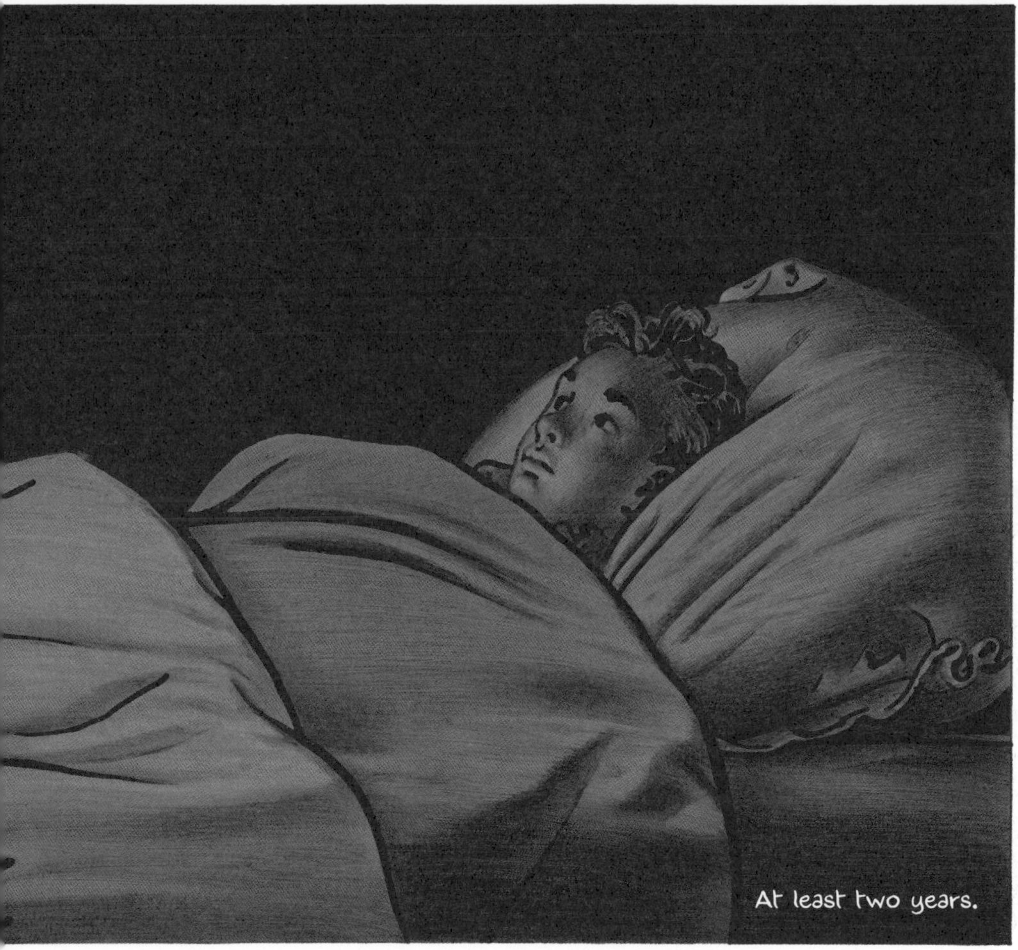
At least two years.

In the months following my mother's death, every Sunday my father would stop in front of a small flower shop, on Pasadena's main street.

Here's some money. Go in and buy a bouquet for your mother.

With the small amount of money he gave me, I'd buy a very modest bouquet. Sweet peas, which were in season, weren't too expensive.

We'd head over to the cemetery where she was buried, in Alhambra.

It was a pretty spot, under a weeping willow.

There was just a small square stone to mark the spot, as a temporary measure.

Later we were supposed to have a headstone installed.

I don't know how long we kept up those visits. Slowly, I suppose, my father got used to his wife's death, and life went on.

There was a lot to do, and we simply stopped going. I'm sure he never put up a headstone.

It's his business.

Maybe he was like me in some ways. He probably thought: "I have to put all that completely behind me, make a new life for myself, remarry; what's the use of putting up a headstone?"

He married Caroline,
the girl who'd come to
take care of the house in the evening.

I think that in the beginning
she just felt sorry for him.
It was obvious that he'd really
loved his wife.

He'd cry now and then;
I felt sorry for him, too.

She was twenty
when they got married.
I was very happy for him.

That whole reaction
I had when my mother died
was pretty odd.
I cried about a lot of things
that made me sad in life,
but not about my mother.
That was too big.
There's a strange kind of beauty
in the way that fate can change
a person's life.
I didn't think it through,
of course.
At eleven, I couldn't think things
through in that way.
It was more of a feeling that I had
in the face of that great tragedy.

That also makes me
think of my reaction
to the enormity of war.
I was never afraid, not one bit.
Except once, when a vehicle
almost ran me over,
but that's another story.
Probably I had an intellectual
kind of fear.
Every day I'd think:
"This could be the last day of
my life."
I'd think it, but it didn't
really scare me because it was
too vast, too natural,
if you know what I mean.

Recently a friend gave me a book by Auguste Rodin.

In it he talks about artists.
I think that I had it in me to be an artist,
but life turned out in such a way that I didn't end up becoming one.
I became what the Germans call "an artistic person."
That's something else altogether.
I'll read you a passage from that book that is deeply meaningful and far-reaching.
Mr. Rodin expresses a feeling very like the one I had at eleven.
The chapter is titled: "For the artist, everything in nature is beautiful."
It's Rodin speaking; he's talking about artists.

"For him, everything is beautiful because he walks always in the light of spiritual truth.

Yes, in the face of suffering, the death of loved ones, even a friend's betrayal, great artists—and by that I mean poets as well as painters and sculptors—are filled with a tragic, ecstatic awe.

Although at times the artist abandons himself to suffering, he experiences, even more deeply than his pain, the bitter joy of being able to comprehend and express it. He is able to discern clearly the hand of fate in all things. He gazes at his own anguish and his deepest wounds with the fervor of a man who has understood the workings of fate. Betrayed by a loved one, he first staggers from the blow, then, his strength returning, comes to view the deceiver as the very embodiment of iniquity and welcomes that act of ingratitude as an experience that enriches his soul. His rapture can be terrifying, but it is joy, too, because it represents an unceasing veneration of the truth.

When he sees beings bent on mutual destruction, youth fading, strength waning, or genius declining, when he comes face to face with the will that has decreed all those dark laws, then more than ever he rejoices in his knowledge and, sated with truth, experiences unsurpassable happiness."

First Second

New York

Originally published in French by L'Association as *L'enfance d'Alan*.

Copyright © 2010, Emmanuel Guibert & L'Association. All rights reserved.
Published by arrangement with L'Association.

L'Asso<iation

English translation by Kathryn Pulver
English translation copyright © 2014 by First Second

Published by First Second
First Second is an imprint of Roaring Brook Press, a division of
Holtzbrinck Publishing Holdings Limited Partnership
175 Fifth Avenue, New York, New York 10010
All rights reserved.

Cataloging-in-Publication Data is on file at the Library of Congress.

ISBN: 978-1-59643-664-0

First Second books are available for special promotions and premiums.
For details, contact: Director of Special Markets, Holtzbrinck Publishers.

FIRST
EDITION

First American edition 2014
Book design by Rob Steen

Printed in China

10 9 8 7 6 5 4 3 2 1

BY ART
WE LIVE